THE COMPLETE GUIDE TO STARTING YOUR OWN CANNABIS BUSINESS

An Introduction to the Medical Marijuana Industry

Martin Samuelson

COPYRIGHT

Table of Contents

Chapter 1- Introduction to Cannabis

Cannabis is commonly known as marijuana in the united states. It is an incredible plant that has helped humanity for many years. The incredible impact marijuana has had on the growth and spread of civilization and conversely, the thoughtful effect humans had on the plant's evolution are now being discovered. Cannabis was known as one of the earliest and most significant plants placed under cultivation by ancient Asian people. Practically, all parts of the plant can be used for many purposes.

From the plant's stem comes hemp, used to make cloths, ropes, and paper due to its very long fiber, and durability characteristic. While dried leaves and flowers from the plant become the euphoriant, together with the root are also useful for medicinal purposes. The seeds were a staple food in ancient China, and was one of their major grains. Cannabis seeds are slightly uneatable and are now used mainly for oil for feeding animals. The oil from the seed is similar to linseed, and is used for paint and varnish making fuel and lubrication.

Cannabis spread □uickly westward from its native Asia and by Roman era, hemp was grown and cultivated in all European countries. Marijuana was the most preferred product in Africa, smoked, and used ritually and also for pleasure. When the first colonists arrived in America, they brought hemp seed with them to make rope and spun cloth. Hemp fiber for ships' rigging was significant to the English navy to the extent that colonists were offered bounties to grow them, and penalties were imposed in some states that didn't. Just before the Civil War, the hemp industry was second only to cotton in the South. Now, cannabis grows all around the world and is considered the most distributed of all cultivated plants, a testimony to the plant's firmness and flexible nature as well as to its usefulness and economic value. Unlike other numerous plants, Cannabis has the ability to flourish even without human help. Anytime ecological circumstances allow, the plants readily "escape" cultivation by becoming weedy and developing "wild" populations. Weedy Cannabis, descended from the long-gone hemp industry, grows in all but more arid areas in the United States. Unfortunately, they usually make an obvious poor grade marijuana.

Such an adaptable plant, introduced into a wide variety of environments, cultivated and grown for a multitude of products, a great number of distinctive strains or varieties developed, each one is uni□ue to suit local needs and growing conditions. A lot of these varieties may be lost through extinction and hybridization unless there is a concerted effort to preserve them.

In the United States, more varieties of marijuana are likely to be cultivated or kept as seeds than any other part of the world. While conventional marijuana growers traditionally grow the same in Asia and Africa, their forebearers grew in a single variety. American growers search for and welcome varieties from all parts of the world. Very powerful, early flowering varieties are particularly valuable because they can reach complete maturity in the northernmost states. The Cannabis stock in the United Nations seed bank is at best, washed-out and in disarray.

Marijuana from 1960 to present day

When you mention marijuana to an average American, you're likely to conjure pictures of people at Woodstock or underage stoners playing in their parents' basements. But cannabis has been used for tens of thousands of years, as both a recreational drug and medicine. Beginning in central and south asia Charred cannabis was discovered in Romanis in a ritual brazier (a bowl or box usually used for burning fuel) that dates back to the third millennium BCE. Ancient mummies have been discovered, from China to Egypt, alongside leaf fragments and seeds, providing signs of cannabis use. Like many herbal and flower products, cannabis usage is an age-old cure.

Cannabis was criminalized not long afterwards in countries around the world , including the United States. First restriction of the drug sale was in Washington, DC, in 1906. In 1937, the Marihuana Tax Act was passed banning manufacturing of the drug. At about the same time, the "dangers" of marijuana use were dramatized in the propaganda film Reefer Madness (originally called "Tell Your Children"), in which formerly clean-cut teenagers get high, hit pedestrians with cars, commit suicide, and eventually go crazy. The counter-culture of the late 1960's embraced marijuana, as we all know from pop culture, and its use became much more widespread.

By the 1970s, state laws and local regulations prohibiting the possession and consumption of cannabis was abolished, due to the Leary v. United States ruling of 1969.

The United States of America deemed the Marihuana Tax Act unconstitutional. Nixon declared the War on Drugs in the

1970s, and called drug abuse "Public Enemy Number One", and classified cannabis in the most stringent category. However, a quarter of the nation had already decriminalized possession by the end of the decade. Nixon expanded the size and scope of federal drug enforcement authorities significantly, and pushed through measures such as mandatory sentences and no-knock warrants.

Nixon temporarily put marijuana on Schedule 1, the most stringent category of narcotics, pending review by a commission he named, headed by Republican Governor of Pennsylvania, Raymond Shafer. In 1972, the commission unanimously proposed that the possession and sale of marijuana be decriminalized for personal use. He ignored the report, dismissing its recommendations.

Yet, 11 states decriminalized possession of marijuana between 1973 and 1977. President Jimmy Carter was inaugurated in January 1977 on a campaign platform that included the decriminalization of marijuana. The Senate Judiciary Committee voted in October 1977 to decriminalize possession of as much as one ounce of marijuana for personal use. Among other political parties, Nixon's private war on drug use and his obsession with marijuana regulations soon lost it's foothold.

The Cheech and Chong comedy pair made a living satirizing the use of marijuana in the 1980s. Their ground-breaking movies helped in building a new public awareness and altered the perspective of a whole generation on "smoking a 'J', "Rolling a Joint," "Doing a Doobie," and the ramifications of marijuana's illegality. This simple-minded comedy shed light on marijuana use at a time when many people in the United States perceived the use of drug as a major offense. Beyond their wildest dreams, their funny irreverent, cynical, pot-smoking culture, no-holds-barred comedy skits about pot-smoking hippies propelled nine hit comedy albums and eight films to number one, smashing box office records, shattering comedy album sales and winning several Grammy awards, confounding fans for over a decade.

Chapter 2 - Legalization of Marijuana

In the mid 1990's, Medicinal marijuana was legalized in California, then shortly afterwards in the state of Washington. Alaska and Maine legalized medical marijuana in the late 1990's. As of this publishing, there are twenty states including Washington, DC, that allowed medical marijuana to be legalized.

On November 6th 2012, Marijuana was legalized in Colorado and Washington for recreational use. People over the age of 21 could possess up to one ounce of marijuana for recreational use in those two states, as well as cultivation of up to six plants.

As of 1 February 2014, the Colorado Revenue Department reported that one third of a million dollars had been raised in taxes related to sales of recreational marijuana stores within the first thirty days of its official opening. Half of those proceeds will go to Colorado's general education fund. This translates into growing taxes from the city and the state as well as allowing the general public to benefit from additional stable jobs: a possible win-win scenario for everyone.

After the legalization of recreational usage in the state of Colorado, with favorable results, the marijuana industry in that state blossomed, and other states and countries for the matter took notice, and it gained popularity, and by all accounts it doesn't seem to be slowing down anytime soon. Lawmakers in states across the country, supported by public opinion and the examples of the success in Colorado and Washington, are putting this issue before their peers, aiming to become the next state to legalize pot. The willingness of legislators in states across the country are partially motivated by the enormous tax revenue that each state might be able to generate from sales of pot from those states.

Legalizing marijuana nationwide could generate tax revenue of at least $132 billion, creating more than one million jobs across the United States over the next decade. There are also other ways in which this new industry could support states in addition to growing revenue from state taxes, such as increasing consumer purchases of goods and services, and most significantly, supporting people with many conditions. Legal marijuana sectors would generate growth in jobs, such as manufacturing, labor, technology, services, and management.

Chapter 3 - Why do you want to start a marijuana business?

There could be many reasons someone might want to start a marijuana/cannabis dispensary business. Maybe a career change, unhappy with their current job, better pay, living out your dream of owning a business, provide a better life for your and your family, etc. Whatever your reason is, do keep in mind it does take some work and effort to start to make any business successful, especially a marijuana business which is not your typical businss.

Since Colorado and Washington legalized marijuana, all of a sudden every entrepreneur under the sun is now interested in opening a businss in this new and exciting industry.

Whether you're starting this type of business in a strong or weak economy, the opportunity is there. Since the marijuana business is so new, the competition isn't as firece as other industries, which makes it a prime business to start.

On of the biggest challenges that you'll face is determining the growth strategy of your business, and what direction you'll want to take your business, and how you plan to scale it beyond your local geographic footprint.

As part of your branding campaign, you'll need to set your business apart from your competitors by having insights and knowledge about the industry that your competition doesn't have. This can be ascertained by talking to experts in the industry about laws, regulations, operational efficiencies, new products, good business practices, etc.

I do need to mention that this business is not for everyone. In the coming pages and chapters, we'll talk about things you will need to think seriously about before making the decision to jump in and start a business in the marijuana industry.

The opportunities are limitless, and so are the risks and the uncertainties that come with being in this industry. The road to success come with obstacles and challenges and rewards if you're willing to take it. Opening a marijuana dispensary businss comes with risk, but what is riskier is a poorly written business plan, and not being able to analyze your risk to reward ratio and ascertaining your risk-bearing capacity to know how much risk you and investors can can bear, and what the upside and reward could possibly be.

Costs to consider

A Marijuana business is not what you would consider a typical business that can you can start with a minimum amount of capital, time and effort. The first thing you have to ask yourself is how much will it cost to start a marijuana dispensary and grow operation. Just like any other business, costs need to be considered, like the cost of the location or space you plan to buy or rent, overhead costs, payroll, inventory, taxes, etc.

Below you will find a list of items that you will need to think about when opening your business:

- ✓ Grow facility equipment and supplies
- ✓ Gardening supplies and equipment
- ✓ City, county and/or state licenses, fees and permits
- ✓ Dispensary furniture and office equipment
- ✓ Legal fees
- ✓ Security rent deposits for dispensary facilities
- ✓ Architectural/engineering plans
- ✓ Computer systems software and equipment (desktop CPU, printer, tablets, internet service, scanner, (POS) Point of sale system, misc. office supplies)
- ✓ Retail displays, fixtures, buildout furniture and cabinets
- ✓ Industrial hygienist certification
- ✓ Equipment (tables, chairs, refrigerator, etc.)
- ✓ Alarm systems for dispensary and grow facility
- ✓ Cameras and monitors for security system
- ✓ Phone systems
- ✓ Sound systems lighting (displays for interior and exterior)
- ✓ Employee lounge
- ✓ Website development, company logo, and print materials
- ✓ Business cards
- ✓ Build-out costs for dispensary and grow facility
- ✓ Reception area furniture
- ✓ Signage for exterior of building
- ✓ T-shirts, hats, uniforms, and other merchandise
- ✓ Electrical upgrades for grow facility to handle higher wattage
- ✓ Miscellaneous equipment and cleaning supplies (towels, mops, vacuum, toiletries, etc.)
- ✓ Marketing and Advertising

- ✓ Business Insurance
- ✓ Initial product order

Chapter 4 - Developing a Business Plan

Selecting a Company name

Selecting the right name for your business can really make a difference in attracting your ideal clientele. A variety of items should represent the name you choose: who you are, what you believe in, and what kind of goods you sell. Above all, it should offer an idea of what to expect and inspire a first-time visitor to come inside and explore. Your initial instinct, could be to give your dispensary a creative funny name with a stoner type theme. Keep in mind, though, that your customer base will be made up of all sorts of people, from seniors seeking relief for chronic pain to returning veterans suffering from PTSD. Your name should reflect that your dispensary is more than a fun time; it is healing, health and nature. Lean to something professional and welcoming, that not only appeals to a number of buyers. Here are some tips on how to pick a name that works in a web-savvy world for your business.

Choose a business name that makes sense

Give some thought to how your name will be used before you choose the name for your business. It is easy to run your company under your personal name if you simply start as a small dispensary. However, you may want to consider the business name you can build with you if you expect long-term business growth. There may be a time when you decide to sell your marijuana company, and having a catchy but professional name will make the sale of your business much easier.

Choose a name that can easily be found on the web

Given that we live in an online world, it makes sense to research whether your business name can easily be found with a simple keyword search on the web. Consider the following:

Search For a domain Name - This lets you decide whether a website with a specifically associated web address (domain name) can actually be established. In the WHOIS database, you can quickly search for a domain name. To find out if the name you have in mind is available, you can do a search on GoDaddy.com. It will let you know whether the domain name you want is available for use or not (e.g. www.hempiness.com) for example. Start the domain name search process early so you can check that item off of your checklist well before you start creating a website. You will have to rethink your name concept if your preferred domain name is not available.

Is your preferred business name e-mail friendly? Make sure the business name is memorable and easy to spell. You might also want an acronym for e-mail purposes for your company name. Additionally, if you or potential employees have long or difficult name to pronounce, come up with a naming convention that includes first and last names (jimdoe@ hempiness.com) or first and last names (jdoe@ hempiness.com) for example.

Is your company name available for social media? In addition to checking your business name 's availability as a possible domain name, take time to search Facebook and Twitter so that no other organization or brands operate with the same name, or a similar name in the social media networking environment.

The name you select will be like the foundation of a building. When the foundation has been put in place, the footing is solid. If its not in place, the building like a business will be misalignment.

Chapter 5 - Establishing a Company Structure

Legal structure for your business

New Company owners will be forced to make a decision as to how to legally set up their business. New company owners need to make a decision and must re-examine their corporate processes as the types of legal organizational structures vary based on city, countym state and federal laws apply and are defined. How much tax you pay, the amount of paperwork your company has to do, your personal responsibility, and the ability to borrow money would be influenced by the kind of business entity you decide to start. In order to make the right decision for your circumstances, you must consider the various market structures.

An accountant or an attorney can help you make the right decision for the future of your marijuana business. The corporate structure which you select will lay the foundation for a legal company. It also covers you in the event of an accident and/or injury to you or to any of your employees, or if a customer or employee is injured or disabled in an accident on your property. If an accident leads to a lawsuit, your personal property could be at risk if they are not adequately protected. You should be covered in these situations by the legal framework you choose for your company. Many new business owners, however, frequently neglect or disregard the need to select a business structure that gives them adequate protection. When deciding on how to legally set up your company, your business and personal security should be at the top of your priority list.

Sole Proprietorship

A sole proprietorship is the probably the most basic and straightforward form of a business organization. It is easy to form, and offers the business owner complete control of the company. It is an unincorporated business owned entirely by one individual and does not require massive amounts of complicated tax forms. An owner who operates with no other employees besides themselves usually chooses a sole proprietorship. This can be a home-based business or one operated out of a retail commercial location.

At a high level, the business owner is also personally liable for all financial obligations, liabilities and debts of the business.

As a sole proprietor, it's always wise to keep accurate and sufficient records, not only for tax purposes, but to track the growth and management of your business. Paying taxes as you can image will be important. Depending on what your accountant advises, you may be able to pay taxes quarterly based on what your estimated payments might be. The estimated tax payments might include both your income tax and self-employment taxes for Social Security as well as Medicare. One advantage of a sole proprietorship is that additional expenses, such as office expenses, property taxes, utilities, and vehicle expenses, may be deducted from the proprietor's income on their personal taxes.

The liability of a sole proprietorship is the full responsibility for any debt, liability, and/or lawsuits that the company might incur. It means that the individual business owner is held personally responsible for damages, problems, or adverse consequences resulting from the operation of the business. The likelihood of you choosing this option to set up your marijuana business is highly improbable. The fact is, in order to operate this business successfully, you will need employees and the protection of a corporate veil. Protection in case of business casualties, changing laws, terminating your lease and/or having to close if the state or city changes its policies on marijuana. A sole proprietorship does not offer this safety.

Partnership

A partnership business arrangement is a business relationship that exists between two or more people who join each other to start a business venture with a common goal, and that is to earn a profit. As part of this partnership, each person makes or contributes money, labor, property, skills, expertise, etc. and expects to share in the overall profits and/or losses of the business venture.

Under most state laws, partners share control over the business equally. You can state in the partnership agreement which partners are responsible for the job duties and responsibilities to which they agree. You may also want to establish voting or proxy rights based on the percentage of the initial investment, or how the amount of work and hours will be distributed among the partners. Your agreement should spell out all of this prior to opening the business. You can specify in your partnership agreement how profits, losses, salaries, and other costs are allocated among partners.

This is also usually based on initial investment and time put into the business. If everyone is equal and puts in the same investment, this agreement becomes very easy. A partnership agreement should also address the eventuality of a partner leaving the business, a partner who is no longer capable of working in the business, the death of a partner, and the addition of new partners.

A partnership is a tax reporting entity, not a tax-paying entity, which means that profits are divided among the partners according to what was agreed to in the partnership agreement.

The partners are responsible for good bookkeeping, paying their tax obligation, Social Security, and Medicare. While there are many benefits to a partnership, one disadvantage is that the owners have unlimited personal liability for their own actions and the actions of their partners.

In general, each partner in the business is jointly liable for the partnership obligations stated in the partnership agreement. Joint liability means that the partners can be sued as a group not individually. Depending on which state you live in, each partner can be held accountable for any damages from the wrong-doing of other partners and for their debts and obligations of the partnership as well.

The three rules for liability in a partnership situation are: 1. All partners are liable for his or her own actions. 2. All partners are liable for the actions of the other partners. 3. All partners are liable for the actions of the employees of the business.

Corporation

Some people might decide that forming a to conduct business might be a good option. Most entrepreneurs aren't comfortable with a sole proprietorship setup, and sometimes need a level of protection not afforded by a sole proprietorship. While some owners think incorporating is only for big companies, the most common form of a business now is to own and operate a business as a corporation.

A corporation is commonly referred to as just a "company." Some of the basic advantages of using a corporation to conduct business include but not limited to the following:

Limited Liability Company: The owners of the corporation are shareholders in the business, and are not liable for the debts of the corporation. Creditors cannot hold the shareholders responsible for the debts of the corporation. If the company cannot pay its debt, the creditors cannot go after the shareholders personally. This is one of the primary reasons why people form a corporation.

Ownership Can Be Easily Transferable: Ownership of a corporation can easily be transferred by transferring the shares od a business. This is done by endorsing the back of the share certificate.

Tax Advantages: If a corporation operates as a small business and has income, then it can take advantage of small business tax deductions and pay income taxes at a significantly reduced rate. There are significant tax savings that you can advantage of if you conduct business outside of a corporation set up. In this case, a corporation would file a separate income tax return. Say for example, a shareholder is an employee with the corporation, he would pay income tax on his wages, and the corporation and the employee each would pay one-half of the Social Security and Medicare taxes and the corporation can deduct half of that. A corporate shareholder only pays income tax for any dividends received.

Raising Capital: In most cases, it's easier to raise capital for a corporation than it is for a partnership or sole proprietor for that matter. Lenders are more willing to lend capital to a corporation that has exibited creditworthiness or has shown to bad a good credit risk. Though currently borrowing money through a bank is not possible for marijuana businesses in today's banking world, hopefully in years to come having a corporation will speed up the lending process when banks and lenders do decide to jump into the marijuana pool.

Limited Liability, Or LLC
A limited liability corporation, also known as an LLC, is a relatively new legal business definition that was formed specifically to provide a host of benefits to new business owners not offered by other entities. Given all the benefits and flexibility of an LLC, business people, lawyers, and accountants now consider the limited liability corporation as the presumptive choice for new business.

Liability Benefits: This corporate setup has some benefits as an LLC, which protects the principles from being personally liable for the debts, obligations, or any lawsuits that may result. The LLC business benefit states that a member is not liable just because he or she is a member or owner of the LLC. There are guidelines that need to be followed by the principals and/or the members of the LLC so this protection is valid. It's important to have a plan to protect your hard earned assets.

Informal Decision Making: In an LLC, the owners determine the ownership structure, the right to the profits, voting rights, and any other aspect of relationships amongst members. An LLC does not require a board of directors, shareholder meetings, and other managerial formalities, which allows the owners to focus more on their business and less on the requirements and maintenance of corporate guidelines and mandates.

Flexible Tax Choices: The tax choices for an LLC are the second biggest benefit of an LLC for small business owners.

The individual member LLC can take advantage of a sole proprietorship federal income taxation benefit, but without the personal liability of the sole proprietorship. What does that mean? As a business owner, you are able to write off all the expenses of a home office, utilities, and car. Usually, you would normally not have the benefit of doing so.

Keep in mind that a single or a multi-member LLC structure can choose to be taxed as a corporation as well. The tax benefits of an LLC provide more choices than other legal entities. When you finally do decide which legal structure is right for your business, it's important to choose the entity that gives you the most protection from personal liability with the best tax advantages for your specific situation.

Chapter 6 - What Marijuana Products Are You Going to Sell

▪ Edibles

Edibles are cannabis-based food products. They come in many different forms, from gummies to brownies, and contain either one or both of marijuana's active ingredients: THC (delta-9 tetrahydrocannabinol) and CBD (cannabidiol).

With the legalization of marijuana, edibles are increasing in popularity. CBD only edibles have been found to help treat ailments such as anxiety and chronic pain. As an added benefit, edibles don't pose risks to the respiratory system, unlike smoking marijuana. Edibles also take longer than smoking or vaping cannabis to kick in, although many factors affect the timing.

Common Forms Of Edibles

Edibles come in many different forms, and new products are introduced into market almost every day. Commom types of edibles include:

- ✓ Baked goods: Brownies, cookies, biscuits, and waffles
- ✓ Candy and sweets: gummies, chewing gum, lozenges, lollipops and hard candy, chocolate, truffles, fruit bars, and marshmallows.
- ✓ Beverages: coffee, tea and iced tea, soda, energy drinks and shots
- ✓ Other products: jerky, butter, sugar, and syrups.

Health Benefits Related To Edible Marijuana

Marijuana has many medicinal benefits, and has been used to treat various ailments throughout history, today, edible marijuana products have a number of uses in the medical field and are becoming a more popular, accepted natural treatment in clinical settings.

May benefit certain health conditions

Edible marijuana products are often used to treat conditions, such as chronic pain, cancer-related symptoms, and anxiety.

■ Bath bombs

For centuries, the benefits of a good hot water soak have been touted as a means of beautification, healing and ultimate relaxation. Now, that is even truer today than it has ever been because of the creation of the Cannabis Bath Bomb. It has been discovered that the cannabinoid CBD has multiple benefits when added to a hot bath.

Health Benefits Of Bath Bombs

1. Relax your mood and boosts mental clarity
2. Help release tension in your body
3. Skin restoration and cell renewal
4. Combat colds and fight the flu
5. Soak away PMS and menstrual cramps

■ Whole Plant Flowers

Cannabis seeds or a whole plant may not be the first thing you think of when you go to the dispensary. Yet, beyond smoking dried cannabis flower, the whole cannabis plant can be used for a variety of functions. Getting to know the plant, beyond just the bud, can help you appreciate cannabis in a new way and from a more holistic perspective. Here are some ways you can utilize it.

1. Make cannabis smoothies

Once your plant is mature and you harvest the bud, don't forget about the leaves! Consuming the leaves of the cannabis plant won't get you high, but will nonetheless become a nutritious addition to your diet. Make juice out of the raw leaves or add them to a smoothie. You'll not only replenish your endocannabinoid system, but you'll reap the benefits of cannabinoids like THCA and CBDA in their raw form, which have anticarcinogenic, anti-inflammatory, analgesic, and antifungal properties.

2. Make a flower bou□uet

Cannabis leaves can be a beautiful garnish to any bou□uet of flowers, and so too, can the cannabis buds if you're looking to give the bou□uet to someone special.

3. You can make cannabis tea

Use can use the leaves and/or the stems to make cannabis tea. It's up for debate whether this will get you high. While THC needs to be heated up to have an effect (otherwise it's just raw THCA), the resin holding the cannabinoids is only fat soluble, meaning that if you steep it in water (without adding, say butter or coconut oil), it won't be as bioavailable. That said, it still may help you relax.

4. Make a topical solution

Grind up the stems, leaves, or even the bud, and other plant material and mix it to a fatty substance like shea butter or coconut oil. Add other herbs like lavender or peppermint and voila, you'll be able to use it to soothe aches and pains.

▪ Cannabis Oils And Waxes

Oil extracts look like a thick, sticky resinous li□uid. They are sometimes called honey oil, due to its gold colour or butane oil due to the solvent used. The extracted cannabis oil from the plant comprises of a number of cannabinoids such as CBD and THC. This concentration is very potent as such it is used to treat a number of medical conditions like epilepsy, anxiety, and inflammatory disease. Medically, it has been tested to impact cancer growth; many have come to agree that cannabis oil will continue to have an impact in the medical community.

Cannabis oil potency level is about 80% more than the cannabis plant itself and its potency depends solely on the amount of tetrahydrocannabinol extracted from the initial plant during the extraction process.

Cannabis oil can also be taken orally through a capsule, an oral syringe or as a drop under the tongue. It can also be mixed with other ingredients while cooking because it has more viscosity than wax, although it should only be prepared with edible solvents such as butter and olive oil for it to be edible.

Cannabis Wax

Also known as crumble, budder and flake extracts are opaque, thick and flaky though moist in nature due to its similarity with beeswax and earwax which results from condensation caused by rapid heating or stirring. It also varies in texture from thick liquid to candle wax. It has a similar extraction process as cannabis oil; the cannabis plant is immersed in a long pipe or tube with butane to extract the THC and making wax through a BHO (Butane hash oil) extraction process.

Unlike cannabis oil, cannabis wax has less potency due to the large amount of wax contained in it making it less potent.

Cannabis can be consumed through a glass called GRAV labs glass or penVAPE, this can be done by placing the extracted wax on a heated pen, and this process allows you to heat your cannabis wax to over 399 degrees with a 4.2 volt battery.

- ## **Pills**

THC is an acronym for Tetrahydrocannabinol, the chemical compound responsible for the psychological effects of marijuana. Commercial THC capsules are made from extracted natural cannabis mixed with natural fatty oils (to facilitate the absorption of cannabinoids by the digestive system). THC pills are often gelatin encapsulated. They also come in the form of softgels, which many refer to as THC softgels.

Health Benefits of Taking THC Pills

There are numerous medicinal benefits that can be derived from THC pills. When consumed, the effect is almost felt immediately. The pill facilitates easier and □uicker absorption of the THC content. Here's a list of some medical conditions which are often treated using THC pills.

1. Arthritis
2. Headaches and Migraines
3. Side effects of chemotherapy
4. Anxiety
5. Depression
6. Sleep Disorders
7. Seizures
8. Pain relief

▪ Vaping Accessories

What Are E-Cigarettes?
Overall, e-cigarettes are battery-powered devices designed to look like a pen, a thumb drive, or even a real cigarette. Some have refillable tanks while others have disposable pods. But regardless of what they look like, they basically all work the same way.

E-cigarettes have containers filled with li□uid that usually contains nicotine, flavorings, and other chemicals. A battery-powered heating device turns the li□uid into vapor, which users inhale when they take a puff off of the device.

Using an e-cigarette is called vaping, although teens refer to using JUULs, a pod-type of e-cigarette, as juuling. Meanwhile, there are hundreds of different types of e-cigarettes on the market, and almost all of them contain nicotine. Sometimes, they even contain THC, the chemical found in marijuana that makes users feel "high."

What You Need to Know About Vaping

Vaping has been around for about a decade now and is growing in popularity, especially among teens and young adults. Originally marketed as a smoking cessation device for traditional smokers to □uit smoking, e-cigarettes are thought to be a safer alternative to smoking.

But, the FDA has not found any e-cigarette to be safe or effective in helping smokers □uit, according to the American Lung Association. In fact, there is some evidence that most smokers today are "dual users," using both cigarettes and e-cigarettes. They simply vape in places or in situations where they cannot smoke like a restaurant or at a friend's house.

What's more, many people assume that e-cigarettes and vaping are safe alternatives to smoking. But that is not the case. Even though some scientists believe they are less dangerous than traditional cigarettes, they are still not a healthy or safe alternative. What's more, vaping is attracting teens and young adults who would not otherwise smoke. So, an entirely new generation of people are becoming addicted to nicotine.

Additionally, several studies indicate that vaping may actually serve as a gateway to smoking, especially among teens and young adults. For instance, a study in the journal, Pediatrics, found that teens who never smoked but started vaping were more likely to try cigarettes than kids who never vaped. Likewise, a study in the Journal of the American Medical Association found a similar connection. They discovered that kids who vape are more likely to smoke cigarettes or other tobacco products over the next year than kids who are non-users.

Interestingly, the CDC states that teen cigarette smoking has dropped to a historic low with just under 15% of teens smoking. However, the use of e-cigarettes went up to 25% in 2015, which represents a dramatic increase in vaping. This increase in vaping has advocates concerned that all the work done to reduce smoking among teens may be undone with vaping. While kids may not be smoking cigarettes, they are vaping in record numbers. Regardless of the method, they are still inhaling nicotine and developing addictions.

The Risks Associated With Vaping

There is a fierce debate about the risks and possible benefits of vaping. Some believe that vaping could help millions of adults quit tobacco cigarettes, while advocates argue that vaping normalizes the habit and lures children into smoking. But those two arguments aside, there is mounting evidence that vaping negatively impacts your health.

Vaping Devices Can Blow Up

Perhaps one of the most shocking risks associated with e-cigarettes and vaping is the risk of explosions and fire from the devices. The shape and construction of e-cigarettes make them more likely to explode than other products with lithium-ion batteries. In fact, when the batteries fail, they behave like "flaming rockets." To help prevent e-cigarette explosions, the FDA recommends that users only purchase vape devices with vent holes. They also suggest replacing e-cigarette batteries that get damaged or wet, and to store loose batteries in a case away from keys and coins.

They also recommend charging vaping devices only with the charger provided and not to charge a vape pen overnight or leave it unattended.

Li□uid Nicotine Can Poison People

Liquid nicotine is especially dangerous to young children, and reports of poisonings are on the rise. Parents and older siblings should be advised to keep e-cigarettes out of reach of small children.

Vaping Is Addictive

Nicotine is a primary ingredient in e-cigarettes, and it is highly addictive. In fact, it is so addicting that without it you will suffer withdrawal symptoms if you try to ignore your cravings. Yet, many people assume that when they are vaping they are ingesting less nicotine than they would be if they were smoking a cigarette. The problem is that some e-cigarettes contain as much or more nicotine than a pack of cigarettes. So, vaping is just as addictive at traditional smoking.

There Are Many Unknowns

E-cigarettes have not been on the market long enough for scientists to determine what long-term use will do to the body.

Plus, e-cigarettes often contain a number of chemicals that are being inhaled into your lungs. At this point, it is impossible to know what those chemicals will do to your body because e-cigarettes have not been out long enough to undergo any extensive studies. Still, many researchers are concerned that the chemicals people are inhaling when they vape may produce conditions like "popcorn lung," which is a type of lung disease caused by the chemical diacetyl. Diacetyl, is a flavor-enhancing chemical that was originally used to improve the flavor of microwave popcorn until it was shown to cause popcorn lung in factory workers.

Chapter 7 - Local, State, Federal and Country Laws on Cannabis

Local, State, Federal and Country Laws on Cannabis

If every word in every law of every state in which medical marijuana is legal were included in this section, the chapter would run to a thousand pages, or more. Instead, the state law highlights are presented here. The synopsis of each state's law provided here, though brief, is highly informative and will point you in the right direction if you are inclined to learn more. Considering the state of the states' medical marijuana laws is akin to placing a frame around confetti after it has gone airborne. The regulations are all over the place. The laws are not uniform at all. Ever. However, there are common characteristics you should consider, themes if you will, which occur as a matter of course in each state's medical marijuana statutory scheme.

However, Cannabis laws in the United States vary widely. Whether an individual caught by law enforcement with a small amount of cannabis will be treated lightly with a small civil fine, or arrested and put through the criminal justice system, depends largely upon one factor: Geographic location. If a cannabis consumer possessing a single ounce of cannabis begins a cross-country automobile journey in Portland, Maine (where cannabis has been decriminalized since 1978), that ounce of cannabis will have changed its legal status dozens of times while crossing the United States on the way to the other Portland in Oregon (where cannabis was first decriminalized in the United States, in 1973). However, if while travelers from Portland to Portland were to interface with law enforcement, and their cannabis were to be lawfully discovered in states such as Indiana, Iowa, Kansas, Utah, South Dakota, or Idaho, then the cannabis-possessing "criminals" would be readily arrested, prosecuted, and face potential incarceration of up to two years.

In Ohio a citizen can possess up to one hundred grams (three and a half ounces) of cannabis and face only a $100 fine, which is treated inconse□uentially as a minor traffic violation. If a cannabis consumer were to be caught in neighboring Indiana with the same amount of cannabis, they'd be promptly arrested and prosecuted as a cannabis dealer based simply on the weight.

Listing Of State-By-State (And Federal) Cannabis Laws And Penalties

Alabama

Possession of marijuana is a criminal, arrestable offense. For possession of an amount of one kilogram (2.2 pounds) or less, the crime is a misdemeanor, punishable by up to one year in jail and a fine of up to $2,000. For possession of any amount over one kilogram, the crime is a felony, punishable by one to ten years in prison and a fine of up to $5,000. The sale, cultivation, or manufacture of marijuana is a felony offense. If the amount is one kilogram or less, the mandatory minimum sentence is three years in prison and a fine of up to $25,000.

The penalties for sale of marijuana are enhanced if the sale takes place within a three-mile radius of a school or public housing project, adding five years to the sentence for the sale. Sale to minors (under eighteen years old) can increase the penalty by ten years to life in prison, and no suspension or probation can be granted to this sentence.

Alaska

Possession of one ounce or less of marijuana in the privacy of a home is legal. The status of possessing an amount between one ounce and four ounces is unclear, pending clarification by the courts. Possession of four ounces or more of marijuana is a felony punishable by up to five years in prison and a fine of up to $50,000.

Any possession within five hundred feet of school grounds or a recreation center, or possession on any school bus is a felony punishable by up to five years in prison and a fine of up to $50,000. Sale, delivery, or manufacture of marijuana of less than one ounce is a misdemeanor and is punishable by up to one year in jail and a fine of up to $5,000. For amounts of one ounce or greater, the crime is a felony that can be punished with a sentence of up to five years in prison and a fine of up to $50,000.

Arizona

The possession of marijuana is a criminal offense. For possession of an amount less than two pounds, the sentence can range from six to eighteen months and a fine of $750 to $150,000. Possession of two or more pounds but less than four pounds is punishable by nine months to two years in jail and a fine of $750 to $150,000. Possession of four pounds or more is punishable by eighteen months to three years in prison and a fine of $750 to $150,000.

The penalties for possession or sale of less than two pounds of marijuana are eighteen months to three years in prison and a $750 to $150,000 fine. For amounts of less than four pounds, the penalties increase to thirty months to seven years in prison and a $750 to $150,000 fine. Possession for sale of four pounds or more is punishable by four to ten years in prison and a $750 to $150,000 fine.

Arkansas

The penalty for possession of one ounce or less of marijuana is a misdemeanor and is punishable by up to one year in prison, and a fine of up to $1,000. The court may defer the proceedings and grant probation for no less than one year. Upon granting probation, the court may re□uire drug treatment. If the terms of the probation are fulfilled, the court can discharge and dismiss the proceedings. There is a rebuttable presumption that any possession greater than one ounce is possession for sale. Possession for sale or cultivation of marijuana is a felony. For amounts greater than one ounce, the punishment is four to ten years in prison and a fine of up to $25,000. For amounts of ten pounds or more the sentence can range from five to twenty years in prison and a fine of $15,000 to $50,000.

California

Possession of 28.5 grams (one ounce) or less of marijuana is not an arrestable offense. As long as the offender can provide sufficient identification and promises to appear in court, the officer will not arrest the offender. Upon conviction of the misdemeanor charge, the offender is subject to a fine of $100.

Possession of greater than 28.5 grams is punishable by up to six months in jail and a fine of up to $500.

Colorado

Possession of one ounce or less of marijuana is a petty offense. The offender receives a summons to appear in court, and upon a promise to appear in court, the offender is to be released from detention. The maximum penalty for a violation is $100.

Failure to appear at the specified time and location results in the increase of the charges to a misdemeanor. Displaying or using marijuana in public results in the added penalty of up to fifteen days in jail.

Possession of greater than one ounce is a misdemeanor, punishable by six to eighteen months in jail and a fine of $500 to $5,000, plus a $600 surcharge.

Transport of greater than one hundred pounds is punishable by eight to twenty-four years in prison and a fine of $5,000 to $1,000,000. Any transfer to a minor is also a felony punishable by two to four years in prison and a fine of $2,000 to $500,000. Any sale within one thousand feet of a school or public housing area increases the penalties to eight to twenty-four years in prison and a fine of $10,000 to $1,000,000.

Connecticut

Possession of up to four ounces of marijuana is punishable by up to one year in jail and a fine of up to $1,000 for the first offense. A subsequent offense is punishable by up to five years in prison and a fine of up to $3,000. Possession of four ounces or more of marijuana is punishable by up to five years in prison and a fine of up to $2,000 for a first offense. Subse☐uent offenses are punishable by up to ten years in prison and a fine of up to $5,000. Possession of any amount within 1,500 feet of a school adds a two-year minimum mandatory sentence to run consecutively with any other sentence imposed.

Delaware

Conviction of any violation involving marijuana allows the court to recommend to the licensing boards within the state that the offender's license to practice or carry on his profession be suspended or revoked. Possession of any amount of marijuana is a misdemeanor, punishable by up to six months in jail and a fine of $1,150. If the possession or sale of marijuana occurs within one thousand feet of a school, the penalty can be up to fifteen years in prison and a fine of up to $250,000, and if it occurs within three hundred feet of a church, park, or recreation area, the penalty can be up to fifteen years in prison and a fine of up to $250,000.

District of Columbia

Possession of any amount of marijuana is a misdemeanor and is punishable by up to six months in jail and a fine of up to $1,000. First-time offenders are eligible for probation and dismissal of the charges upon successful completion of the probation contract. The cultivation, sale, or delivery of any amount of marijuana is punishable by up to one year in jail and a fine of up to $10,000. If the distribution occurs within one thousand feet of a school, pool, playground, arcade, library, youth center, or public housing, or if the distribution is made to a minor, the penalties can be doubled.

Florida

Possession of twenty grams or less of marijuana is a misdemeanor, punishable by up to one year in jail and a fine of up to $1,000. Possession of greater than twenty grams of marijuana is a felony, punishable by up to five years in prison and a fine of up to $5,000. The delivery of twenty grams or less of marijuana for no consideration is a misdemeanor and is punishable by up to one year in jail and a fine of up to $1,000. Sale, delivery, or cultivation of any other amount up to twenty-five pounds is a felony and punishable by up to five years in prison and a fine of up to $5,000.

Sale, delivery, or cultivation of greater than twenty-five pounds is considered trafficking, and all trafficking offenses have mandatory minimum sentences.

Georgia

Possession of less than one ounce of marijuana is a misdemeanor and can be punished by up to one year in jail and a fine of up to $1,000. However, upon a first drug conviction, the offender may be placed on probation, and upon successful completion the proceedings against him may be discharged. Possession of one ounce or more is a felony and is punishable by one to ten years in prison. Any cultivation, manufacture, or distribution is a felony, punishable by one to ten years in prison.

Hawaii

Possession of less than one ounce of marijuana is a misdemeanor offense, punishable by up to thirty days in jail and a fine of up to $1,000. Possession of one ounce or more is a misdemeanor punishable by up to one year in prison and a fine of up to $2,000. Any possession of amounts of one pound or more are felonies.

The possible sentence for possession of one pound or more is up to five years in prison and a fine of up to $10,000. Possession of two pounds or more is punishable by up to ten years in prison and a fine of up to $25,000. Possession of twenty-five pounds or more is punishable by up to twenty-five years in prison and a fine of up to $50,000.

Any marijuana found in a vehicle results in all the occupants of the vehicle being charged with its possession, unless the marijuana was found on the person of one of the occupants.

Idaho

It is a crime to be under the influence of marijuana in a public place or to use marijuana in a public place, punishable by up to six months in jail and a fine of up to $1,000. The penalty for possession of three ounces or less of marijuana is up to one year in jail and a fine of up to $1,000. Possession of greater than three ounces is a felony and punishable by up to five years in prison and a fine of up to $10,000. The penalty for cultivation, sale, or distribution of less than one pound (or fewer than twenty-five plants) is a prison term of up to five years and a fine of up to $15,000. Cultivation, sale, or distribution of amounts greater than one pound are all subject to mandatory minimum sentences. The maximum possible punishment for any cultivation, sale, or delivery is fifteen years in prison and a fine of up to $50,000.

Illinois

Possession of 2.5 grams or less of marijuana is a misdemeanor, punishable by up to thirty days in jail and a fine of up to $1,500. Possession of greater than 2.5 grams is punishable by up to six months in jail and a fine of up to $1,500. Possession of greater than ten grams is punishable by up to one year in jail and a fine of up to $2,500. All possession of greater than thirty grams is considered a felony.

Indiana

The possession of thirty grams or less of marijuana is a misdemeanor punishable by up to one year in jail and a fine of up to $5,000. For first offenders, the court may consider a conditional discharge. For possession of more than thirty grams, the penalties range from six months to three years in prison and a fine of up to $10,000. The cultivation, delivery, or sale of thirty grams or less is a misdemeanor, punishable by up to one year in jail and a fine of up to $5,000. Cultivation or delivery of more than thirty grams is a felony, punishable by six months to three years in prison and a fine of up to $10,000.

Iowa

The possession of any amount of marijuana is a misdemeanor, punishable by up to six months in jail and a fine of up to $1,000. For a second offense the penalties increase to up to one year in jail and a fine of up to $1,500. Subsequent offenses are punishable by up to two years and a fine of $500 to $5,000. There is the possibility for conditional discharge for possession charges. Possession within one thousand feet of a school, public park, swimming pool, or recreation center adds an additional one hundred hours of community service to the sentence.

Kansas

Possession of any amount of marijuana for personal use is punishable by up to one year in jail and a fine of up to $2,500. For a second conviction the penalty increases to ten to forty-two months in jail and a fine of up to $100,000. Possession with intent to sell or actual sale is punishable by fourteen to fiftyone months in jail and a fine of up to $300,000. Probation is possible for sentences of less than thirty-two months. Sale or possession with intent within one thousand feet of a school is punishable by forty-six to eighty-three months in prison and a fine of up to $300,000.

Kentucky

Possession of less than eight ounces of marijuana is a misdemeanor, punishable by up to one year in jail and a fine of up to $500. For subse□uent offenses, the penalties increase to one to five years in jail and a fine of $1,000 to $10,000. Possession of eight ounces or more is considered possession with intent to sell and is charged as trafficking. Sale or delivery (trafficking) of less than eight ounces is punishable by up to one year in jail and a fine of up to $500. The penalties for sale or delivery of eight ounces or greater are one to five years in prison and a fine of $1,000 to $10,000. Sale or delivery of five pounds or more is punishable by five to ten years in prison and a fine of $1,000 to $10,000.

Louisiana

Possession of any amount of marijuana is punishable by up to six months in jail and a fine of up to $500 for a first offense. For a second offense the penalties increase to up to five years in prison and a fine of up to $2,000. A third or subsequent offense increases the penalty to up to twenty years in prison. Cultivation or sale, or possession with intent to distribute less than sixty pounds of marijuana is punishable by five to thirty years in prison and a fine of up to $50,000.

Maine

Possession of less than 1.25 ounces is a civil violation, punishable by a fine of $200 to $400. Possession of a usable amount of marijuana is lawful if at the time of the possession the person has an authenticated copy of a medical record demonstrating that the person has a physician's recommendation. Cultivation of five plants or less of marijuana is punishable by up to six months in jail and a fine of up to $1,000. For more than five plants, the penalties increase to up to one year in jail and a fine of up to $2,000. For more than one hundred plants, the possible punishment is up to five years in prison and a fine of up to $5,000.

Maryland

Possession or use of any amount of marijuana is punishable by up to one year in jail and a fine of up to $1,000. Cultivation, delivery, or sale of less than fifty pounds of marijuana is punishable by up to five years in prison and a fine of up to $15,000. For fifty pounds or more, the penalties increase to a five-year mandatory minimum sentence and a fine of up to $100,000. If the sale occurs within one thousand feet of a school, while the school is in session, or on a school bus, the penalty is up to twenty years in prison and a fine of up to $20,000.

Massachusetts

Possession of one ounce or less of marijuana is a civil offense, subject to a $100 fine like a traffic ticket. Offenders under eighteen will be required to attend a drug-awareness program or pay a $1,000 fine. Possession of more than one ounce of marijuana is punishable by up to six months in jail and a fine of up to $500. For first-time offenders, the court will sentence the offender to probation, and upon successful completion of the probation period, the offender's record will be sealed. For subsequent offenses, probation may still be possible. Cultivation, delivery, or sale of less than fifty pounds of marijuana is punishable by up to two years in prison and a fine of up to $5,000.

Michigan

The penalty for the use of marijuana is up to ninety days in jail and a fine of up to $100. Possession of marijuana in any amount is punishable by up to one year in jail and a fine of up to $2,000, unless the possession occurred in a public or private park, which increases the penalty to a possible two years in prison. Conditional discharge is available in all use and possession cases. Distribution of marijuana without remuneration is a misdemeanor, punishable by up to one year in jail and a fine of up to $1,000. For cultivation of less than twenty plants or sale of less than five kilograms, the punishment is up to four years in jail and a fine of up to $20,000.

Minnesota

The penalty for possession of a small amount (less than 42.5 grams) of marijuana is a fine of up to $200 and possible re□uirement of drug education. Possession of 42.5 grams or more of marijuana is punishable by up to five years in prison and a fine up to $10,000. Possession of ten kilograms or more of marijuana increases the penalty to a fine up to $250,000 and up to twenty years in prison.

Possession of greater than 1.4 grams in a motor vehicle (except in the trunk) is punishable by up to one year in prison. Conditional discharge is a possibility for first-time offenders.

Mississippi

Possession of thirty grams or less of marijuana is punishable by a fine of $100 to $250 for the first offense. For possession of greater than thirty grams, the penalty increases to a fine of up to $3,000 and up to three years in prison. The penalty for possession of 250 grams or more is two to eight years in prison and a fine up to $50,000. For possession of five hundred grams or more, the penalty is six to twenty-four years in prison and a fine up to $500,000. For possession of five kilograms or greater, the penalty is ten to thirty years in prison and a fine up to $1,000,000.

Missouri

Possession of thirty-five grams or less of marijuana is a misdemeanor, punishable by up to one year in jail and a fine up to $1,000. Possession of greater than thirty-five grams is a felony and is punishable by up to seven years in prison and a fine of up to $5,000. Possession of greater than thirty kilograms is considered trafficking and the penalty is five to fifteen years in prison. Possession of one hundred kilograms or more carries a penalty of ten years to life in prison. Sale or manufacture of five grams or less of marijuana is a felony, punishable by up to seven years in prison and a fine of up to $5,000.

Montana

Possession of sixty grams or less of marijuana is a misdemeanor, punishable by up to six months in jail and a fine of $100 to $500 for the first conviction. For subsequent convictions, the penalties increase to up to three years in prison and a fine up to $1,000. Possession of greater than sixty grams carries a sentence of up to twenty years in prison and a fine up to $50,000.

Nebraska

Possession of one ounce or less of marijuana is an infraction, and the offender receives a citation and is subject to a $100 fine and possible referral to a drug education course for the first offense. For a second offense, the penalty increases to a possible five days in jail and a fine of $200. For subsequent offenses, the fine increases to $300 and a possible seven days' jail time. For possession of greater than one ounce, the penalty is up to seven days in jail and a fine up to $500. Possession of greater than one pound is punishable by up to five years in prison and a fine up to $10,000.

The penalty for distribution of marijuana is up to twenty years in prison and a fine up to $25,000. The penalty increases for sale to minors and sale within one thousand feet of a school, college, or playground, or within one hundred feet of a youth center, public swimming pool, or video arcade to the next-higher classification of offense.

New Hampshire

Possession of any amount of marijuana is a misdemeanor and is punishable by up to one year in jail and a fine up to $2,000. Manufacture or distribution of less than one ounce of marijuana is punishable by up to three years in prison and a fine up to $25,000. For one ounce or more, the penalty increases to a possible seven years in prison and fine up to $100,000. Manufacture or distribution of five pounds or more is punishable by up to twenty years in prison and a fine up to $300,000. Penalties for sale or distribution within one thousand feet of a school are up to two times the possible prison term and fine. Upon conviction of a person aged fifteen to eighteen years for possession with intent to sell, an additional penalty of one-to five-year driver's license suspension may be imposed.

New Jersey

Possession of fifty grams or less of marijuana or being under the influence of marijuana is a disorderly persons offense, punishable by up to six months in jail and a fine of up to $1,000. Possession of greater than fifty grams is punishable by up to eighteen months in jail and a fine of up to $25,000. Any possession within one thousand feet of a school adds an additional one hundred hours or more of community service to the sentence. Manufacture or distribution of less than one ounce of marijuana is punishable by up to eighteen months in jail and a fine up to $10,000. For amounts of one ounce or more, the penalty increases to three to five years in prison and a fine up to $25,000. Manufacture or sale of five pounds or more or cultivation of ten to fifty plants is punishable by five to ten years in prison and a fine up to $150,000.

New Mexico

Possession of one ounce or less of marijuana is a petty misdemeanor, punishable by up to fifteen days in jail and a fine of $50 to $100 for the first offense. For subsequent offenses, the penalty increases to a possible one year in jail and a fine of $100 to $1,000. Possession of greater than one ounce is punishable by up to one year in jail and a fine of $100 to $1,000. For possession of eight ounces or greater, the penalty increases to up to eighteen months in jail and a fine up to $5,000. For a first offense, manufacture or distribution of one hundred pounds or less of marijuana is punishable by up to eighteen months in prison and a fine up to $5,000. For subsequent offenses, the penalty increases to a possible three years in prison and a fine up to $5,000. For amounts greater than one hundred pounds, the penalty can be up to three years in prison and a fine up to $5,000.

For distribution of greater than one hundred pounds within a drug-free school zone, the penalty increases to up to nine years in prison and a fine up to $10,000 for the first offense and up to eighteen years in prison and a fine up to $15,000 for subsequent offenses.

New York

Possession of twenty-five grams or less of marijuana is punishable by a fine of $100 for the first offense. For the second offense, the penalty increases to a $200 fine, and for subse□uent offenses the fine increases to $250 and a maximum of fifteen days in jail time may be imposed. Possession of greater than twenty-five grams or possession of any amount in public where the marijuana is burning or open to public view is a class B misdemeanor and is punishable by up to three months in jail and a fine up to $500. For possession of greater than two ounces, the penalty increases to a possible one year in jail and a fine up to $1,000. Possession of greater than eight ounces increases the penalties to a possible one to one-and-a-half years in prison and a fine up to $5,000.

North Carolina

Possession of one-half ounce or less is punishable by up to thirty days in jail, most likely suspended. Possession of greater than one-half ounce is punishable by one to 120 days in jail, with a possibility of community service or probation in lieu of jail. Possession greater than 1.5 ounces increases the penalties to up to twelve months in jail. Manufacture, cultivation, sale, or delivery of less than five grams for no remuneration (payment, barter, or exchange of any kind) is considered possession and not sale. For amounts of ten pounds or less, the penalty is up to twelve months in jail.

North Dakota

Possession of less than one-half ounce of marijuana is a misdemeanor, punishable by up to thirty days in jail and a fine of up to $1,000. Possession of one-half ounce or more is punishable by up to one year in jail and a fine of up to $2,000.

First convictions for possession of one ounce or less of marijuana can be expunged from the record after two years if no further criminal violations occur. Possession of greater than one ounce of marijuana is punishable by up to five years in prison and a fine up to $5,000. Possession of less than one-half ounce while operating a motor vehicle is punishable by up to one year in jail and a fine of up to $1,000. Sale, distribution, or manufacture of less than one hundred pounds of marijuana is punishable by up to ten years in prison and a fine up to $10,000. For amounts of one hundred pounds or more, the penalty increases to a possible twenty years in prison and a fine up to $10,000.

Ohio

Possession of less than one hundred grams of marijuana is a citable offense only, with a fine of $100. Possession of one hundred grams or more is punishable by a fine of up to $250. For possession of two hundred grams or more, the penalty increases to a possible sentence of six months to one year in jail. Possession of one thousand grams or more is punishable by one to five years in prison. Any possession of less than five thousand grams does not carry the presumption of prison, which leaves available the possibility of probation. Possession of five thousand grams of marijuana or more is punishable by one to five years in prison.

Sale or distribution of less than two hundred grams carries a penalty of six to eighteen months in jail. Sale or distribution of two hundred grams or more is punishable by one to five years in prison.

Oklahoma

Possession of any amount of marijuana is punishable by up to one year in jail for the first offense and two to ten years in prison for subse☐uent offenses. Conditional discharge is available to first-time offenders. Cultivation of one thousand plants or less is punishable by two years to life in prison and a fine up to $20,000. Cultivation of greater than one thousand plants is punishable by twenty years to life in prison and a fine up to $50,000. Sale or delivery of less than twenty-five pounds is punishable by two years to life in prison and a fine of $20,000. For sale or delivery of twenty-five pounds or more, the penalties increase to four years to life in prison and a fine of $25,000 to $100,000. Any sale to a minor doubles the penalties. Sale within two thousand feet of schools, public parks, or public housing doubles the available penalties and carries a mandatory minimum sentence of 50 percent of the imposed sentence.

Oregon

Possession of less than one ounce of marijuana is punishable by a fine of $500 to $1,000. Possession of one ounce or more is punishable by up to ten years in prison. Conditional discharge is possible for possession offenses. Possession of greater than 110 grams is considered a commercial drug offense and penalties are substantially greater, depending on the prior record of the offender. Delivery of less than five grams, for no remuneration, is punishable by a fine of $500 to $1,000.

Pennsylvania

Possession of thirty grams or less of marijuana is a misdemeanor, punishable by up to thirty days in jail and a fine of up to $500. The penalties for possession of greater than thirty grams increase to a possible one-year prison term and a fine up to $5,000. Delivery for no remuneration of thirty grams or less of marijuana is treated as possession with a possible penalty of thirty days in jail and a fine up to $500. Cultivation, delivery, or sale of one thousand pounds or less is punishable by up to five years in prison and a fine of up to $15,000.

Rhode Island

Possession of less than one kilogram of marijuana is punishable by up to one year in jail and a fine of $200 to $500. Driving while in possession of marijuana is penalized by suspension of the offender's driver's license for six months for the first offense and for one year for subse☐uent offenses. Manufacture or delivery of less than one kilogram of marijuana is punishable by up to thirty years in prison and a fine of $3,000 to $100,000. Delivery to a minor at least three years younger than the offender adds an additional two to five years in prison and a fine up to $10,000. Sale or possession within three hundred yards of a school, public park, or playground doubles the possible penalties.

South Carolina

Possession of one ounce or less is punishable by up to thirty days in jail and a fine of $100 to $200 for a first offense. For subsequent offenses the penalties increase to up to a year in jail and a fine of $200 to $1,000. Convictions for a first offense are eligible for conditional discharges. Possession of greater than one ounce is considered evidence of intent to sell and is punished as such. Sale or delivery of less than ten pounds of marijuana is punishable by up to five years in prison and a fine up to $5,000.

South Dakota

Possession of two ounces or less of marijuana is a misdemeanor and is punishable by up to one year in jail and a fine up to $1,000. Possession of less than eight ounces is punishable by up to two years in prison and a fine up to $2,000. For less than one pound, the penalty increases to a possible five years in prison and a fine up to $5,000. Possession of ten pounds or less carries up to ten years in prison and a fine up to $10,000. For amounts over ten pounds, the penalty is up to fifteen years in prison and a fine up to $15,000. A positive urine test or other evidence of recent marijuana use is considered possession and is punished as such. Inhabiting a room where marijuana is being stored or used is punishable by up to one year in jail and a fine of up to $1,000.

Tennessee

Possession, delivery, or sale of one-half ounce or less is punishable by up to one year in jail and a fine up to $2,500. For delivery or sale of amounts over one-half ounce the penalty increases to one to six years in prison and a fine up to $5,000. Delivery or sale of ten pounds or more is punishable by two to twelve years in prison and a fine up to $5,000

Texas

Possession of two ounces or less of marijuana is punishable by up to 180 days in jail and a fine up to $2,000. Possession of greater than two ounces is punishable by up to one year in jail and a fine up to $4,000. For greater than four ounces, the penalty increases to 180 days to two years in jail and a fine up to $10,000. Possession of greater than five pounds carries a penalty of two to ten years in prison and a fine up to $10,000.

Any sale to a minor is punishable by two to twenty years in prison and a fine up to $10,000. Sale within one thousand feet of a school or within three hundred feet of a youth center, public pool, or video arcade increases the penalty classification to the next highest level

Utah

Any conviction results in a six-month driver's license suspension. Possession of less than one ounce of marijuana is punishable by up to six months in jail and a fine up to $1,000. For possession of one ounce or more, the penalty increases to up to one year in jail and a fine up to $2,500. Amounts of one pound or more carry a penalty of up to five years in prison and a fine up to $5,000. Possession of greater than one hundred pounds is punishable by one to fifteen years in prison and a fine up to $10,000.

Vermont

Possession of less than two ounces of marijuana is punishable by up to six months in jail and a fine up to $500 for the first offense. For a second offense the penalty increases to a possible two years in prison and a fine up to $2,000. There is a possibility of deferred sentencing for first offenders. For possession of two ounces or more, the penalty is up to three years in prison and a fine up to $10,000. Possession of one pound or more is punishable by up to five years in prison and a fine up to $100,000. Cultivation of more than twenty-five plants carries a penalty up to fifteen years in prison and a fine up to $500,000. Sale or delivery of less than one-half ounce of marijuana is punishable by up to two years in prison and a fine up to $10,000.

Virginia

Possession of marijuana is punishable by up to thirty days in jail and a fine up to $500 for the first offense and up to one year in jail and a fine up to $2,500 for subseΠuent offenses. Cultivation of marijuana is punishable by five to thirty years in prison and a fine up to $10,000. A conviction for manufacturing marijuana must include proof that the marijuana was being grown for a purpose other than the grower's personal use. The delivery or sale of one-half ounce of marijuana or less is punishable by up to one year in jail and a fine up to $2,500.

Washington

Possession of less than forty grams is punishable by up to ninety days in jail and a fine up to $1,000. For amounts of forty grams or more the penalties increase to up to five years in prison and a fine up to $10,000. Cultivation, delivery, or sale of marijuana is punishable by up to five years in prison and a fine up to $10,000. Any sale to a minor at least three years younger than the offender doubles the possible penalties.

West Virginia

Possession of marijuana is punishable by ninety days to six months in jail and a fine up to $1,000. Possession with intent to manufacture or deliver a controlled substance is a felony and can result in imprisonment of not less than one year and not more than five years, or a fine of $15,000 dollars, or both. Conviction of possession of less than fifteen grams triggers an automatic conditional discharge. Conditional discharge does not apply to a defendant who has previously been convicted of any offense relating to narcotic drugs or marijuana.

Wisconsin

Possession of marijuana is punishable by six months in jail and/or a fine of $1,000 for the first offense, and for second or subsequent offenses (includes any prior controlled substance conviction), three-and-a-half years in jail and a fine of $10,000. Conditional discharge is available for first offenders. Possession within one thousand feet of a school, school bus, public park, public pool, youth center or community center adds an additional one hundred hours of community service to the sentence for possession.

Wyoming

Using or being under the influence of marijuana is punishable by up to ninety days in jail and a fine up to $100. Possession of three ounces or less of marijuana is punishable by up to one year in jail and a fine up to $1,000. Possession of greater than three ounces carries a penalty of up to five years in prison and a fine up to $10,000. Any possession within five hundred feet of a school increases the fine by $500. First offenders may be placed on conditional probation and may have the proceedings discharged. Cultivation of marijuana is punishable by up to six months in jail and a fine of up to $1,000.

Chapter 8 - What Type of Cannabis Facility do You Plan to Operate

How to pick the right location to grow your facility

If you are successful and able to secure a license to operate in the industry, the first □uestion is, how do I pick the right location? What do I look for? Picking the right location is extremely important. If you make a mistake with the wrong spot, you may be forced later to move your whole operation at and it might be costly. The first step is to approach your local municipality, visit the city clerk's office and ask if any land or business ones have been designated as areas for the cultivation and medical or recreational sales of marijuana.

Your city may have a certain part of town where they want your business to be located. There might be restrictions on how many marijuana businesses are able to operate in town and how far apart. Each municipality is different; it's up to the city council to establish what they want in their community, so it's important for you to know what they are thinking. They make the rules that you will need to follow. If they have decided to allow dispensaries to open anywhere, it's up to you to choose the right location.

The federal government enforces a distance requirement, which must be adhered to in looking for a location. The most important factor in picking your location is to be at least one thousand feet away from any public or private school, university, or day care center. This regulation also applies to certain businesses such as liquor stores and adult bookstores.

The federal government still considers marijuana an illegal controlled substance, so stay away from any government-owned buildings. You might also want to stay away from hospitals and places of worship, just to be safe.

In most cases, you are looking for two locations; one for the dispensary and the other for the garden or grow. The best and most efficient way to pick the perfect spot is to have both operations under one roof. Your dispensary is in the front and your cultivation center in the back. This is not easy to find because of the zoning differences for manufacturing/cultivation centers and retail type businesses. Opportunities for this type of operation are more available outside city limits in the county where the building you rent/own has no zoning restrictions.

This location makes an ideal business model because of the ease of management in having everything under one roof. Theoretically speaking, you are actually running two businesses at the same time. Both are open seven days a week, both have different personnel, and both have completely different operating procedures. If your garden is located an hour away from your dispensary, you have more travel time involved in addition to the business itself, which is very time consuming. If you are looking to work forty hours a week in the beginning to start this business, this might not be for you. Be prepared to work every day, ten to twelve hours or more, if you want to be successful in this business. If you aren't able to get everything under one roof, then the next best thing is to have your dispensary and garden as close to one another in the same municipality as possible. Remember that both of these operations are open seven days a week. Try to make it easy on yourself to go back and forth between the two facilities to manage your business effectively.

Your garden (grow location) is where the crux of your entire business is, so stay attuned to what's happening with your crop. There have been instances of a garden destroyed by insects in as short as a week. If the subtle changes in the plants have gone unnoticed, the whole crop could have been lost. If you have no crop, you will be forced to buy from another dispensary or grower. Buying from someone else reduces your profit margin dramatically, and depending on the size of the garden, it could mean hundreds of thousands of dollars in lost revenue. As a startup, you can automate your grow and view operation online with digital video monitoring technology, but it will dramatically increase your initial financial investment. It really comes down to how much or how little of an investment your want to make.

Here is what to look for when searching for a Grow location.

First and foremost, check with your municipality for "zoned" areas. Once that is established, here are some pointers to look for in the grow area:

What is the amount of electricity coming into the space? Most of the time you will have to increase the amount of electricity coming into your location. For example, a 100 light operation needs approximately 800 amps of power to run. For a location that is about 5000 square feet for example, a normal warehouse would use a 200 amp panel.

Is there enough power coming into the building? In most cases no, so you will have to look at the transformer designated to your building and see what other parts of the building are being covered by this. If you check with your electric utility company, you can see how much is dedicated to your building. Is there enough air conditioning? This is critical in any indoor operation. Imagine each light is 1000 watts of power, that creates a lot of heat, and multiply that by 100. It gets very hot!!

The bottom line is that you will need a lot of air to keep your environment at the right temperature. The rule of thumb is one ton for every three lights unvented. Unvented means that most hooded light systems are vented from the outside with air to cool the bulbs so they aren't creating a lot of heat. If you are venting your lights, it would be one ton for every five lights. If you were putting in a 100 light operation, I would recommend 30-40 tons. If your landlord covers this, it will save you a lot of money. Rent a building away from others with little or no foot traffic.

Marijuana has a very strong smell and the odor will leak outside the building. If detected, it presents an opportunity for theft and possible air □uality violations. Make sure that your building is well lit. If not, add lighting where needed. A cement or cinder block built warehouse is the preferred style of construction to rent. Buildings constructed of a metal or aluminum siding are less secure and less efficient for indoor environmental conditions. Look for a landlord who wants a long-term lease. Space is very limited and real estate is at a premium.

Many municipalities ban the industry all together and won't allow you to rent/own and operate gardens in their town. Look for warehouse space that has empty space available next to it. This will be important later for expansion. Some cities will allow you to expand if there is empty space connected to your existing location connected by a common dividing wall. This would allow you to use your existing license for expansion and not have to apply for a new one, which probably won't be available.

What a Plant Needs to Survive Indoors

When it comes to choosing an indoor area to start a grow in, there are a few essential things that need to be considered to ensure the area can provide everything a grow space needs.

Temperature and Humidity: Cannabis plants are comfortable in the same indoor temperatures and humidity that people like, so typically, most indoor areas do not have to worry much about this. However, if you are planning to grow in an uninsulated area, such as a garage, basement, or attic, you will need to figure out a way to keep the grow setup close to room temperature throughout the entire grow cycle.

Fresh Air (flow): Ideally, you want the grow space to be able to pull in fresh air from the outside, but pulling air from another indoor space that has a window will work as well. For example, if you are growing in a closet that is pulling air from a room with an open window, that is enough for the plants to breathe. Fresh air is only half the equation, though, as a light breeze towards the plant is equally as important. Often times, this is as simple as positioning an intake fan towards the plant or adding a clip-on fan to a grow setup.

Size: The size of the grow space, especially the height, will dictate a plant's maximum size. Ideally, you want at least 4 feet of height for a small grow to thrive and 6 feet of height to maximize a plant's potential. Remember that around 2 feet of space is always taken up by the pot and grow light.

Light: Speaking of lights, the size of your light will need to match the grow space in size, and every light type also has their pros and cons, as well as distance required away from your plants. It is important to understand the basics of each type of grow light available to make a better decision on what light is the best option for your grow situation.

Enclosure: While it is always possible to grow a plant in an open indoor space enclosing the grow provides a plethora of benefits. From reflecting the blinding grow lights during the day cycle to ensuring no light leaks out during the night cycle, enclosing the plant allows for more control. With a smaller enclosed space, air movement is easier to control and smells are easier to contain.

Smell: Cannabis only has a faint smell until it starts to flower, but once it is in the flowering cycle, the distinct odor can easily spread throughout an entire house, so if that is going to be an issue, you will need to either mitigate the smell by exhausting the grow space air outdoors or by completely scrubbing it from the air with a carbon filter, both of which will require more initial planning and setup.

Electricity: This one is a little trickier to figure out because you will not only need to access the electrical box but also know which fuse is linked to the wall outlet(s) you want to use. After that, you will need to add up all the electrical draw from everything plugged into the outlet and then see if that is near or exceeds the wattage limit for your AC outlet.

After choosing an indoor area to start the grow, it is time to convert it into a grow space.

Indoor Grow Space

There are three common ways to enclose a grow space: using a space that is already enclosed, like a walk-in closet; using a prebuilt enclosure, a grow tent; or building a DIY enclosure with things such as buckets or storage totes.

A closet grow is the first go-to space for most people because a lot of the initial work is already done. The area is enclosed, the grow space is concealed, and if you have white paint and solid floors, the walls already reflect light and the floors are semi water-resistant. For most closet grow setups, the issues come from what it does not provide: mobility, fresh airflow, mounting bars, and a way to control the odor.

The question now is how hard is it to add on what is missing from the grow space, and depending on things such as where the nearest window is, a closet could be your ideal grow space. Another thing to consider for long-term growing is that the interior of a house is not meant to handle a high level of humidity and water spills, so peeling paint and mold are both possibilities that could occur with a lack of planning.

A grow tent is one of the most popular choices because of the low price point, ease of setup and high versatility. Grow tents come in multiple shapes and sizes, with the smallest viable option. A 2'x2'x4' is recommended being the largest ones able to fill a whole room. For a home grower, anything larger than 4'x4'x8' is probably more than you will need if you are growing for personal use. Built with metal bars that click together, these tents are a breeze to put together and take apart, making them easier to put together than basically any other option. The biggest benefit of a grow tent, though, is the ease of use; all the necessary features of a good indoor grow setup are already built into the tent.

A DIY enclosure such as as pace bucket,brute bucket, or space tote, makes sense for growers with a limited space that require a custom fit. Otherwise, you might be better off starting with a grow tent because they cost about the same and require a lot less work to set up. Space buckets are the most common DIY grow setup; they are 5-gallon buckets stacked on top of each other with a grow light at the top of it to house and grow a plant. The space-saving, lightweight durability from the hard shells of the buckets make this type of setup very mobile and able to fit in places grow tents can not, making these common as a go-to option when it comes to micro and stealth grows. The cons, though, are that because of its shape and size, a typical space bucket will only be able to grow one very small plant at a time and require the grower to have a good understanding of a few different grow techniques to keep the plant short since a space bucket can only stack so high. The larger versions of a space bucket, using trash cans (brute bucket) or plastic storage containers (space tote), can grow more plants at once but require more space to do so, so they are not as common, as they can usually be interchanged with a grow tent for the same cost..

Finally, a standalone grow cabinet is another popular DIY enclosure, taking a normal storage cabinet and retrofitting it so that it has all of the tools a grow space needs, making it essentially a customizable but costly grow tent. For people looking to grow long term who want something more durable, this is a good alternative. When compared with the rest of the options, this one has the hardest initial setup, since everything a grow tent automatically has built in will need to be added manually.

Grow Lights

Now that your grow space is enclosed, we can take a look at grow light options. In the crowded field of different grow light technologies, there are 3 main types that make the most sense for a grower starting out: light-emitting diode (LED) lighting, high-intensity discharge (HID) lighting, and fluorescent lighting.

LED growlights are a great starting point for a new grower due to their low cost, ease of setup, and high efficiency, while producing very little heat. The problem is that these lights are also the most confusing of the bunch as they come in all shapes, sizes, and colors, but we will be focusing on the two most common types available.

Blue/red LED grow lights, also known as blurple grow lights, are the most common grow light on the market with hundreds, if not thousands of variations. Generally the cheapest grow light available, these work surprisingly well for their price point as long as you know what to look for, and do not get scammed by marketing ploys.

Blurple LEDs have a lot going for them as they are cheap, energy efficient, bright, and produce little heat, but the light they produce is not very intense and will not penetrate far past the first layer of growth, so the lower layers of growth will drop considerably. Even with this drawback, blurple grow lights are a great choice for any new grower looking to start on a budget.

The newer LED technology, chip on board or COB grow lights condenses the LEDs into a smaller area, which produces a stronger penetrating light that can reach further down into a plant. These generally are full spectrum, creating a more natural light for your grow space, and they are usually more correctly labeled to match their actual wattage, although be sure to check the descriptions to make sure.

Now, as for what size of LED grow light you will need, you generally want around 6-10w of LED lighting for every cubic foot of your grow space with the low end of the wattage for partial tent coverage and the high end of the wattage if you are filling the entire tent. For example, a 2'x2'x4' grow space that has 16 cubic feet could use a LED grow light that produces 96−160 actual watts.

HID grow lights such as metal halide (MH) and high-pressure sodium (HPS), are extremely popular due to their dominance in the grow light market before LEDs came out in the market. Both MH and HPS lighting are used throughout a plant's life cycle because MH lights emit more blue lighting, which promotes growth in the vegetative stage, while HPS lights are used in the flowering stage, as they emit more red lighting, which helps with flowering. If you're on a budget, HPS lighting can also be used in the vegetative stage to cut down on the number of setups needed.

Fluorescent lights, while not as commonly used as HID and LED grow lights, have a few uni□ue features that give them a niche role. Fluorescent lighting generates very little heat and produces a low-intensity light. Because of these two characteristics, fluorescent lighting will need to be placed in close proximity, inches away from a plant, to be effective.

Air(flow)

When it comes to an exhaust fan, to keep the plants happy, you want to be able to refresh all the air in your grow space every minute of the day. To determine this, you will need to multiply the length, width, and height of your grow space. For example, a 3'x3'x6' grow tent will need to move 54 cubic feet of air per minute (CFM), so any fan rated 54 CFM or higher will work. Unfortunately most basic fans do not come with a CFM rating, so to give you an example, a small 120mm fan in a personal computer can easily move 100 CFM. This means that basically any small fan that can fit in your exhaust vent will work as an exhaust fan. Exhaust fans also have another role of removing the hot air generated from the grow lights, so when installing one, you will need to position it as high up as possible since heat rises.

Intake fans are generally not necessary since an exhaust fan will naturally pull in fresh air as it removes air from the grow space — just be sure fresh air can come into the grow space, ideally near the bottom, so the fresh air travels through the entire grow space before it exits via the exhaust fan at the top.

As for creating airflow through the plants, any small fan will do. For a small grow space, a clip-on fan is a popular choice.

Carbon Filter and Other Optional Tools

A carbon filter is by far the best solution available to remove the cannabis odor from an indoor grow area, and while it looks intimidating, a carbon filter is actually very easy to setup and requires no real maintenance once installed. All you need to do is to place the carbon filter on one of the 2 ends of the exhaust fan setup: either attached to the exhaust fan inside the grow tent so that all the air pulled in goes through the carbon filter first, or at the end of the ducting outside the grow tent so all of the air is pushed out of the carbon filter. Either way works, and as long as the exhaust air passes through a carbon filter at some point, it will completely scrub the cannabis smell from the grow space. Be sure to check periodically to make sure the smell is being scrubbed, as a carbon filter needs to be replaced every 6–24 months, depending on the level of use.

Outdoor Grow space

Ideally, you will want the plants to be in an environment that is not too hot and not too cold (60–90°F), not too dry but not too humid (40–60% relative humidity), and with enough sunlight in the spring and summer months to support a vegetative stage (over 12 hours) and less sunlight in the fall and winter months to trigger the flowering stage (under 12 hours). If your outdoor environment meets most or all of these requirements, then outdoor growing is a great option due to its biggest benefit: natural sunlight.

With sunlight, there is more than enough lighting to support a plant from all angles, which produces a plant that will grow more evenly in the vegetative stage and side stems that will produce more yields in the flowering stage when compared to indoor plants which typically only fully develop the parts of the plant that are closest to the grow lights. This also makes training techniques typically unnecessary, making outdoor plants easier to work with. Also, outdoor plants do not have the same height restriction indoor plants have. When coupled with an extended vegetative stage, this can produce huge plants during each grow season that can not be matched with an indoor setup.

However, if any of the key environmental ranges listed above are off, it usually takes a lot more work, effort, and money to correct than it would with an indoor setup. Growing outdoors also increases the risk of abiotic and biotic issues, from dealing with unpredictable weather, such as heat waves and snow storms, to bugs and animals eating the plant.

Finally, without additional e□uipment, you will only have one grow season a year, unless you utilize automatic seeds. If you are growing off-season with automatic seeds or with additional equipment such as an outdoor grow light, you will still need to ensure a favorable grow environment in the off-season months to support a healthy vegetative and flowering stage.

Building an outdoor grow space

Unlike an indoor grow space, growing outdoors requires nothing but access to the sun, so all the tools we cover are optional to adjust the outdoor environment to better suit the plant growth.

Adjusting the Environment

Since there is no way to change the weather, any major environmental adjustments will re□uire the plants to be enclosed for the grow to be effective. However, before needing to enclose your plants, there are a few simple but less-effective ways to slightly adjust a plant's environment. Placing your plant under the shade in hot environments, covering your plant with a frost blanket and using thick insulated clay pots in cold environments, blowing air on to your plants with a fan to combat high humidity, and misting the leaves of your plants with water to combat low humidity all help to offset slight variances in the environment.

Greenhouse Options

Starting with the cheapest option, there is a basic plastic enclosure that can be homemade with something as simple as a few plastic pipes and a clear plastic polyethylene sheet. For those who do not want to build one from scratch, pre-made plastic enclosures are also cheap to buy in all shapes and sizes as well, making these a good option for a few plants for one or two grow seasons. For something sturdier than plastic, there are a ton of options to choose from, and these will vary in price based on the size, features, and materials used to make them, but for the price and quality, a polycarbonate panel greenhouse is our favorite choice for multi-year use. No matter what you choose, just make sure the greenhouse is at least 6 feet tall, as outdoor plants can naturally grow that high with a typical spring-to-summer vegetative stage.

Once the plants are enclosed, a lot of tools become effective in controlling the environment. The first tool every enclosure needs is a humidity and temperature reader, and be sure to buy one that is rated for outdoor use too. To ward off heating issues, a shade cloth on top of the greenhouse (which comes in different percentages to control how much light you want to let through) and an exhaust fan installed at the top of the enclosure are the simplest options, followed by evaporative coolers and portable air conditioning units for more extreme heating issues.

For combating the cold, insulating the greenhouse with bubble wrap is good enough to keep the plants nice and warm, although portable heaters can also be used against the extreme cold if needed. Humidifiers and dehumidifiers can help with any humidity issues, and since the enclosure blocks out the outside wind, be sure to get a fan blowing on the plants to keep them healthy and strong.

Pest Control

Other than fluctuations in the environment, the biggest risk with growing outdoors is a constant exposure to bugs. While indoors, this is easy to control, outdoors, there is always a risk of some harmful pest making your plant its home. So, preventative measures should always be taken when working with an outdoor garden. The most common way to do this is to have a bi-weekly organic spray rotation to prevent any harmful bugs from nesting on the plants, and what you use will depend on what type of bugs you normally have in your region.

Outdoor lighting unlike indoor lighting, which needs to be very intense for the cannabis plants to grow has a different purpose, which is to extend the sunlight hours of the day to keep a plant in the vegetative stage when growing off season.

Seed

Cannabis seeds are what most new growers will be starting a grow with. Here we will take a look at how they are made and where to obtain them.

How a Seed Is Made

Cannabis seeds are traditionally created from a male and female cannabis plant. In the flowering cycle, a male plant creates pollen in pollen sacs, and when the pollen sacs are fully developed, they open up, spreading the pollen around, which will pollinate any nearby female flowers. From this point, a seed will be fully developed in the female flowers in about 1–2 months. While that is how most seeds are produced, there is an exception to this, and that is from hermaphrodite plants.

Due to either genetics, external stress, or certain chemicals, female cannabis plants can create their own pollen sacs, which can pollinate itself as well as other female plants. Because the seeds created this way have no male genes, all the resulting seeds will grow to be female plants as well, which is how feminized seeds are created. However, based on how the hermaphrodite plant came to be, the seeds it produces could have a chance of becoming a hermaphrodite plant as well, which would make these seeds terrible for bud production, but as long as the parent plant started with good genetics and became a hermaphrodite through the right processes, the odds of her seeds becoming hermaphrodites are much lower.

As for the different types of cannabis seeds available, there are two categories of seeds and then two types for each category. The Photoperiod "normal" seeds and the Ruderalis "automatic" seeds are two species of cannabis that have different growing traits due to their lighting requirements, and then there are regular seeds and feminized seeds for each of those species. In terms of what to look for in a healthy seed, although each different strain of cannabis has seeds that could look slightly different from each other, the rule of thumb is that if the seed is firm and dark in color, then it is mature and ready for germination. If it is lighter in color and soft, then it is underdeveloped and probably won't sprout. This is, of course a generalization and useful only if you are making your own seeds. If buying seeds, as long as you are buying from a trusted source, you should expect that, no matter what the seeds look like, they are ready to germinate.

In terms of where to buy seeds, if you have access to a local dispensary, some will have seeds for sale; otherwise, there are a lot of reputable seed banks online. For unused seeds, you want to store them in a dark, cool and dry environment. Cannabis seeds will germinate when in contact with moisture in a warm environment, so by preventing both, it ensures the seed can be stored long-term. In general, seeds can last for a few years if stored properly, although the longer they are stored, the lower the odds of germination.

Chapter 9 - Leasing Space and What to Expect

Negotiating the Best Lease

Now could be one of the best times ever to negotiate a great commercial lease for your business. Since the downturn of the economy, we have seen a huge decrease in commercial shopping center occupancy. Some shopping and strip malls are only fifty percent occupied with tenants. Landlords are looking for any opportunity to lease their locations, and they are offering incredible deals to fill their empty spaces. This creates a huge opportunity that would normally cost you much more. The key is to know what to look for and what questions to ask. Keep in mind that your rent will be one of the largest fixed expenses you have every month. The importance of negotiating this lease agreement will help better manage your budget and financial outlook.

Basic Lease Cost

The first item of business you and your landlord will need to discuss is how much you will pay for rent. Usually, your monthly rent will be determined based on the square footage of the space, which is calculated at a per square foot cost. If you multiply width times the length of the space, then multiply your answer by the dollars per square foot, that will give you your base yearly rent. Example 20' length x 20' width is 400 square feet. As an example, a predetermined square foot price negotiated with landlord is $15 per square foot. Multiply your 400 (square feet) x 15 (dollars per square foot) = $6000. Now divide $6000 by 12 (months). This will give you your monthly rent: $6000/12 = $500 a month.

Additional Costs

Sometimes you will have additional costs to figure into your monthly rent expense, called CAM (common area maintenance), or triple net. It is often an addition to the monthly rent or an annual assessment per tenant. The CAM includes the maintenance of any common areas, like walkways, landscaped places, parking lots, and in some cases, restrooms. It is common for the landlord to include CAM charges in the rent price of your commercial lease if negotiated correctly. Getting the most out of your leased space is often determined by the market conditions of your location.

Repairs & Improvements

These are a critical part of your lease negotiations. The build-out in your garden can be very expensive. Ideally, if the previous tenant was a cultivation facility, changes could be minimal; however, this usually only occurs after a few years of operating in a state. Three important factors to consider: The amount of electricity coming into your location and the amount of power coming into the whole building. The size of the air conditioners and heating units, and the size of the transformer for the building. This information will help you determine how much you will need to add to run the operation effectively.

Free Rent

It's important in the first year to negotiate a very low rent to allow you to turn a profit quickly or utilize your dollars elsewhere, such as in advertising and marketing. You might be able to negotiate six months free rent in the beginning or half rent. There are many ways to be creative when it comes to leases. Especially if the landlord is eager to rent a space. Free rent can be very helpful in the beginning stages of setting up your business. The overall expense of setting up a dispensary and / or grow facility is not cheap. Although you may hit the ground running due to the success of other marijuana businesses, knowing that your rent is prorated or not having to pay for the first few months will enable you to absorb the startup costs and get started without the burden of a rent expense.

Reasons why free rent is so important:

- Construction time, including permits, plus it takes about 3 to 4 months fro approvals on city and state levels in a best case scenario.
- Free rent during this building process (no revenue at this point) will be very helpful.
- Training your staff and incurring payroll expenses as the business is being built.
- Leaving your other employment while building your new business. You'll need money to pay your bills.
- Running your grow operation until it produces revenue; it will be a four-month minimum until you harvest.
- You will be paying laborers to garden. Upfront expenses, such as building out your grow operation and/or dispensary.

Details Of Your Commercial Lease Negotiations

Issues to address in your lease: Acceptable signage is detailed. What happens if you need to relocate? So, what if someone wants to buy your business? Can they take over the lease? What happens if you outgrow your space? What happens if you want to downsize? What happens if you go out of business? What happens if the Federal government shuts you down? All great questions to ask and know the answers to ahead of time.

Final Steps—Legal Advice

As a final precaution, take the lease documentation to an attorney who specializes in lease agreements. You can never be too careful about signing a commercial lease. Your lawyer will alert you to any red flags, answer your questions, and explain exactly what you are signing. Due to the fact that the marijuana business is new, the feds have the right to shut down your dispensary business under the U.S. Controlled Substance Act and can shut your business down for any reason. Also, the state can shut you down as well. Please keep all these things in mind.

Chapter 10 - Business Financing and Working Capital

So you've decided to jump on the legal marijuana train. In the old days, a gold miner could talk an investor into what was called a "grubstake," where the investor would fund the miner and take a share of the profits. However, that was then and this is now. The normal channels to secure start-up money from financial institutions and the Small Business Administration (SBA) are probably not going to be viable options any time soon. It is highly doubtful the federal government will ever allow the SBA to authorize loans for what they consider an illegal substance business.

In case you were wondering just exactly how much you will need to start your business, be prepared: you will probably need in the neighborhood of between $200,000 to $1,000,000+ to get into the legal business of owning and operating a marijuana dispensary and/or grow facility depending on the state you live in. No, that is not a mistake in the zeros. You need to consider some of the following necessities your capital will purchase: all of the permits (city and state), retail space rent, electric, water, alarm systems, software, computers, equipment, display cases, inventory, employees, etc. You may have all the skills, education, drive and personality it takes to create a successful business, but without financing, your dream of owning a legal marijuana business may only be pie in the sky. But where there is a will, there is always a way. The amount of money you will need will depend on the business you are thinking of starting.

To open a marijuana dispensary and/or grow operation, money is essential, and the capital needed to get started is not minimal. There are many factors to consider when opening either of these operations. The capital needed up front and ongoing for the first year is substantial. The ability to bankroll this business will be one of the largest obstacles to getting started and continuing your new marijuana business.

Find Funding On The Internet

The Internet has revolutionized how businesses find start-up money. Numerous sites offer advice regarding how to put together a business plan and connect with various sources that can help you find the financing you need. Investigate financial firms that specialize in ac□uiring investors.

Family & Friends

This is another viable start-up source. Family and friends can give you money on the basis of how well developed your business plans is put together. This removes bank paperwork (bank loans are not available at this time, but could be in the future), credit approval and bank fees.

Don't be afraid to approach or ask for their time, attention and consideration. The worst they can say is, "no thanks." This business opportunity is new, and increasing numbers of people are considering options in the industry. They may not immediately want to jump in, but they will listen to a good sales pitch.

The following alternatives may also enable you to accomplish your dream: How much cash do you have in your bank account(s)? What assets can you sell? (Cars, jewelry, gold, silver, anti□ues, etc.) Do you have a stock or investment portfolio you can leverage? Can you draw equity from real estate or a home you own?

Credit Cards

Today over fifty-four percent of businesses use credit cards in some manner to get up and running. They provide instant cash and the interest can be used as a legitimate deduction on your tax return. But realistically, how much of a balance or limit do you have? The downside is the high interest rates most credit cards carry might put you in a hole with no way out. This is not the ideal way to start a business, but it may be the only way to get the money to at least start you on the right path of business ownership.

Life Insurance Policy

If you have a whole life insurance policy with at least three years of maturity, you could obtain a loan against the cash value. Most insurance companies will lend up to 90 percent of the policy's cash value at rates generally more reasonable than those charged by credit card companies.

Retirement Funds

If you still have full-time employment, check into the possibility of taking money out of your 401k plan. Rules may vary from company to company, but you can generally follow these guidelines: If you are older than 59½, you can take out your entire portfolio without any penalties and just pay income tax on the amount you withdraw.

If you are younger than 59½, you will be charged a ten percent penalty on the amount you withdraw and also have to pay income tax on the amount at well. This may be one of your only options for raising the money to open your marijuana business. Remember though, this money would have been used for your future retirement.

Home Equity

If you own your home or income property, you can obtain a home equity loan or a second mortgage. Most financial institutions will allow you to borrow as much as eighty percent of your property's equity. Be mindful though: if you borrow against your home and your business fails, the bank will not hesitate to foreclose on your home. Many of us don't have the luxury to borrow against our homes due to the fluctuating real estate market.

Social Media and Online Funding

A large number of people belong to various social media sites and groups. These types of sites have proved to be viable resources for practically everything under the sun. You may have to get very creative in order to find your start-up money, but it is entirely possible that you could create your own consortium of investors via the social media network. Contact current owners of legal marijuana businesses and pick their brains. A few popular webite funding sources that you could try are......www.gofundme.com, www.crowdfunding.com, www.kickstarter.com, and www.indiegogo.com.

Leasing

Leasing sources can accommodate all applicants for financing, whether you have been in business for twenty years or are just starting out. Leasing programs give you flexibility to finance your furniture, equipment and installation. There is usually a seventy-four hour turnaround from application to receiving an answer. The leasing company does not put liens on your assets, so this may be a worthwhile alternative. The payments are fixed and not subject to fluctuations with an increase in interest rates (as opposed a loan). Leasing does not require a large down payment; you can expect to put down ten percent, or even less for the equipment as a security deposit. This leaves you with more working capital for other expenditures for your business.

Future Financing

One thing to keep in mind: with the legalization of marijuana, and the federal government stating they will not prosecute these types of businesses, banks will eventually feel secure enough to start accepting deposits from, and eventually make loans to, cannabis stores and growers. Once banks recognize the potential profits to be made from loan transactions, they will allow business people to go through the same loan application process just like any other business. Don't hold your breath waiting for that to happen anytime soon though. Your best course of action is to fund your business through private resources and investors.

Chapter 11 - Dispensary Business Operations

When you're caught up in the excitement of starting a new business, it's easy to ignore the need for license and permits. However, license and permits are mandatory, and before you can legally begin to put a seed in a soil pot or try and sell marijuana you will need to have licenses and permits in place. Additionally, if your business has employees and will sell taxable goods (hopefully plenty of marijuana), you need to register with the state and federal taxing authorities and regulatory agencies. Businesses licenses, permits, and tax registrations are issued and administered by all levels of government, federal, state, and local, including county and municipal government as well.

Your state/municipality will require licenses and permits for your dispensary/grow facility. The State of Colorado was used as an example of what you are likely to be expected to obtain. Other states/municipalities may have different requirements, so make sure you have everything before you submit the forms and write the checks for submission. Do not fill out these forms incorrectly! This chapter is designed to walk you through the business licensing process which will help eliminate the possibility of errors, costly re-filing fees, lost time and aggravation.

Medical Marijuana Establishment
License Procedures for a Business Seeking Licensing
Licensing authorities must be provided with the following information in order to move to the production system licensing procedures. The following information will create

both the electronic and hard file documents for the establishment. A business seeking licensing for A Medical Marijuana Establishment must first do the following.

Submit all required documentation to the Department of Excise and Licenses Required Documents. Please see list below:

- Application Lease or Deed-if property is leased
- Written consent from the owner of the property to the licensing of the premises for a Medical Marijuana Establishment
- Certificate of Good Standing from the Colorado Secretary of State Office (For this example used)
- Articles of Incorporation or partnership and any trade name filing
- Description of products and services to be provided.
- Floor plan-drawn to scale on 8 ½" x 11" paper, showing the layout of the establishment and the principal uses of the floor area, including where any services other than dispensing of medical marijuana are proposed to occur.
- Security plan indicating how applicant will comply with security provisions listed in the ordinance.
- An area map-drawn to scale on 8½" x 11" paper, indicating the radius of one-quarter mile from the boundaries of the property upon which the establishment is located, the proximity to any school, pre-school or child care establishment.
- Zone Use Permit Copy of City Sales Tax license Copy of Burglar Alarm Permit Copy of contract with alarm monitoring company
- Affidavit of Lawful Presences FEES Sec. 32-93.

Applicants will be given an Inspection Card from Excise and Licensing. The applicant is responsible for contacting the agencies listed on the card and securing all approvals. Once all inspections are complete, the applicant should contact Excise and Licensing for the final inspection.

The applicant will be notified, in writing, if the application is disqualified or the license is denied for any of the following reasons:

- ✓ Incomplete application
- ✓ False information
- ✓ Lack of possession of the premises
- ✓ Failure to pass inspection by any agency inspecting the premises
- ✓ Failure to comply with spacing requirements.

Applicants whose application has been denied shall be entitled to a hearing on the application upon written request to the appropriate agency. Any application that contains incomplete information shall be denied. Any application denied merely because the application was incomplete may be resubmitted.

Occupational license

This section will walk you step-by-step through the occupational license process. These types of licenses are re□uired by your state/municipality for all employees of Medical Marijuana/Personal Use, Marijuana dispensaries and grow facilities. The State of Colorado is used in this example; check with your state and obtain the correct forms. Make several copies and practice filling them out. Any mistake will void this process and you will have to resubmit a correct form and probably have to pay a new filing fee each time. Make sure they are filled out correctly!

Occupational License Applications are accepted Monday - Friday Between the hours of 8:00 AM and 12:00 PM and 1:00PM and 2:30 PM at MED Head□uarter Office 455 Sherman Street, Suite 390 Denver, CO 80203 "We make every effort to accommodate all applicants on the day of their arrival. Occupational License Applicants will NOT be processed after 2:30 p.m." State statute and rule mandates that anyone working within the Medical Marijuana industry be licensed by the MED (Marijuana Enforcement Division) in order to ensure that they meet specific statutory re□uirements (C.R.S § 12-43.3-307; C.R.S. § 12-43.3-202 (2) (VIII) and C.R.S. § 12-43.3401 (1) (d)).

IMPORTANT
These statutory re□uirements include:
- Applicants must be age twenty-one or older, Applicants may not have any Controlled Substance Felony Convictions or any other felony convictions that have not been fully discharged for five years prior to applying.
- Applicants may not have any delinquent governmental or child support debt, AND Applicants must be a Colorado resident at the time of application. Therefore, all occupational license applicants must undergo a background check, the depth of which is dictated by the level of the individual's involvement in the business.

The two types of Occupational Licenses available are for "Key Employees," and for "Support Employees."

Key Employees

This license is for employees who make operational or management decisions that directly impact the business. An example of such an employee is a master grower who determines what or how much of a particular strain to produce, or an individual whose decisions have a significant impact on the business and its operations, but does not have an ownership interest in the business. Note that two years of a tax background check is required before an approval of an occupational license.

Support Employees

This license is for employees who work within the business but do not make operational decisions. An example of such an employee would be a budtender. The majority of occupational license holders are in this category. All applicants initially applying for an occupational license must come into a MED office to submit their application, have their fingerprints taken and pose for a photo that will be placed on their occupational license badge. If they pass the background check, the information provided on the application is used to determine if the applicant meets the statutory criteria. Key Occupational Licenses cost $250 and Support Occupational Licenses cost $75; this cost reflects the level of scrutiny necessary to obtain the license.

Come Prepared

When applying for your license be sure to bring your completed application (Key or Support), all supporting documentation (such as tax documents, proof of residency or court dispositions), and the full amount of your application fee. They cannot accept credit cards so the fee must be paid in cash or with a check made out to the MED or the Colorado Department of Revenue. The application fee covers the cost of conducting the necessary background check, and is based on the amount of investigation necessary; Key Occupational Licenses cost $250 and the Support Occupational license costs $75. Once you have received your occupational license, keep in mind that by completing the application you have entered into an agreement to advise the MED, in writing, of any criminal conviction or charge pending within ten days of any arrest, summons or conviction. Additionally, you must advise the MED of any change in your home address should the MED need to contact you. This is especially important when the time comes to renew, as the MED will send any renewal information to this address.

Occupational License Renewal

Sixty days prior to the expiration date of your occupational license, the MED will notify you via First Class mail, sent to the home mailing address of record with the MED, the home address you provided at the time you applied for the license or any updated address you have provided to the MED.

This notification will consist of a renewal packet intended to provide the MED with the necessary information to confirm that you still meet the statutory criteria allowing you to hold an MED Occupational License. Complete and sign the application, attach any necessary supporting documentation re□uested and mail the completed packet and your renewal fee to the MED office. If your application is approved the MED will mail you a renewal sticker to place on your badge/identification card. If you fail to pass the background check you will have an opportunity to re□uest a meeting to resolve any issues that arise. If you choose not to pursue this option you must return your expired badge to the MED and discontinue your employment within the Medical Marijuana industry.

NOTE

If your mailing address has changed it is your responsibility to notify the MED of your address change, you can do this by letter or email. Provide your full name, badge number, your previous address and your current address, along with the date you moved.

Individuals wishing to upgrade a Support Occupational License to a Key Occupational License will need to complete a Key Occupational License Application and come into the MED Office in order to complete the in-depth background check necessary. Support badges cannot be upgraded to Key badges via the mail-in renewal process.

Finding the right location for your dispensary

It is said the three most important decisions you will make are location, location, and location. If you are creating and building your dispensary, or even relocating or opening a second location, then the details of the location might not be the first thing on your mind, but they should be. Put location on the top of your list as the single most important factor for your new business.

Your amazing concepts, business ideas, services, products and the best marijuana in your area will go unnoticed if you do not take the time to do your homework and pinpoint the perfect location. Your location is a huge factor in how you market your business, determine which products to carry, and set prices. Your location says a lot about you, your business, your brand, and the customers you wish to attract. Here are several key factors that you should consider when choosing a location for your dispensary and or grow operation. You must keep in mind that once you have met your city and state regulations on areas that have been approved for marijuana, you should follow these principles for selecting the best locations:

Population & Your Customer

Begin by researching the city and area you have selected for your medical marijuana business thoroughly before making a final decision. Read local papers and speak to the small business owners in the region. Ask them the difficult questions regarding their business: What unexpected expenses, like taxes and fees came up when they started their business here? Is the Chamber of Commerce active in promoting new businesses? Are they open to a marijuana operation in their area, and will they help promote your new business? Is the city or county good at repairing the streets, sidewalks, etc. on which your business will be located? Obtain location demographics online, or through the local Chamber of Commerce and/or the Census Bureau. The best advice you will receive is from the local coffee shop or restaurants in the neighborhood. Observe the people: how do they dress, where do they shop, when are people shopping, and are they buying or browsing?

Accessibility, Visibility, & Traffic

Don't confuse a lot of traffic for a lot of customers. Your marijuana business wants to be in a location where there are many shoppers, but only if the shopper meets the definition of your target market. Small retail stores may benefit from the traffic of nearby larger stores. When considering visibility, look at the location from the customer's viewpoint.

This CHECKLIST will give you more insight on picking your location:

- ✓ How many people walk or drive past the location in a given day, week or month?
- ✓ Is there public transportation in the loca area?
- ✓ Can clients easily get in and out of the parking lot?
- ✓ Is there adequate parking spaces?
- ✓ Is there adequate fire and police presence in the community?
- ✓ What is the crime rate in the neighborhood or surrounding are?

- ✓ Can the store be easily seen from the main road or highway?
- ✓ Will the dispensary's sign be visible from afar?

Signage, Zoning, & Planning

Before you sign a lease or purchase agreement, be sure you have a full understand all the rules, policies, and procedures related to your business location. You can call your local city hall and zoning commission for information on regulations regarding the space you are interested in renting. The planning board determines the correct use for the location. Although the landlord may love the idea of having a full service dispensary and grow operation in that location, the planning board will have the final say on whether or not it is allowed. It may also be a good idea to ask the planning officer about signage and regulations. Many towns are very sensitive about the height and the type of signage allowed.

Competition & Neighbors

When choosing your location, it is a good idea to see how many dispensaries are in the same vicinity as the location you are interested in. If this is a new area opening up for medicinal or recreational marijuana, you most likely may be the only one in that area. Other types of businesses may help or hurt your business. The key is to be next to a retailer that draws other people to the area. Schools and hospitals are out of bounds. You will have a 1,000 square foot red flag on these types of properties. Being next to a busy coffee shop or designer store may be fantastic to give you instant exposure.

Small Town Or Big City?

There aren't many options in small municipalities, because they limit the area and the amount of dispensaries, so take what you can get and hope you don't get taken advantage of. In large cities, there are more opportunities, but you need to do your homework and get in front of the most desirable locations. Marijuana-zoned areas can become as pricey as beach front real estate.

Location Costs

Besides the base rent, consider all the costs involved when choosing your marijuana business location. These costs will be your monthly overhead no matter what else arises: Lawn care, building maintenance, utilities, and security upkeep and repair of the heating/air conditioning units, property taxes (depending on the lease), water and sewer costs, and insurance on the property and contents.

Personal Factors

The marijuana business requires you to be there every day. When choosing a location, it is important to think about your commute. How far would the business be from your home and other things you do on a daily basis? Do you need to take children to school? How close is your bank? How far is shopping? The commute can easily overshadow the exhilaration of your new business if you are spending a lot of time traveling to and from work. Commuting has the potential to stifle your independence.

Questions That Will Make Or Break Your Location

Most people focus their energy on the creative side of the new business and neglect some important aspects of choosing a location. Answering these □uestions for the site you are considering will help you determine if you have chosen the right location for your new business:

CHECKLIST: Check off the □uestions below as you get answers.

- ✓ Is the facility located in an area that is zoned for a marijuana business?
- ✓ Is the facility large enough for your business?
- ✓ Does it meet your layout re□uirements?
- ✓ Does the building need repairs?
- ✓ Does the building have a crawl space or basement for easy access to utilities?
- ✓ Are the lease terms and rent favorable?
- ✓ Is the location convenient to where you live?
- ✓ Can you find □ualified employees in the area?
- ✓ Does the location have the customers you are looking for?
- ✓ Is this a seasonal community?
- ✓ Does the area have the image you are looking for?
- ✓ Is this a safe neighborhood?
- ✓ Is there exterior lighting on the building?
- ✓ Will local businesses attract clients to your business?
- ✓ Are there many competitors nearby?
- ✓ Can suppliers make deliveries conveniently at this location?
- ✓ Is the parking adequate for the dispensary?
- ✓ Is the area served by public transportation?
- ✓ Can potential clients see the location at night?
- ✓ Will there be walk-in business?

- ✓ Is the building insulated? Is there enough electricity coming into the building?
- ✓ In case of robbery or fire is there a police and/or fire department in the area?

Chapter 12- Medical Marijuana – What You Need to Know

Medical marijuana is a plant-based medicinal product from the species of the Cannabis sativa or Cannabis indica with three main active compounds: THC, CBD and CBN. Normally, when people bring up the topic about medicinal marijuana, they talk about how the marijuana plant is used to treat health issues. Many people do use medical marijuana to treat their medical symptoms.

Cannabis, when sold legally is sold as a medicine for differnet types of medical symptoms and ailments. Here are a few that are thought to provide health benefits.

Medical marijuana is used for:
- ✓ Pain
- ✓ Nausea
- ✓ Muscle spasms
- ✓ Anxiety
- ✓ Multiple sclerosis
- ✓ Low appetite
- ✓ Sleep problems
- ✓ Autism
- ✓ Epilepsy (seizure disorders), and other conditions

Benefits are seen in immune function, neuroplasticity, regulation of emotions and moods, vascular health and digestive function. Research studies indicate that some advantages may include neuroprotection (in MS, epilepsy, other movement disorders), and benefits in a variety of mood and anxiety disorders. Medical marijuana's side effects are mild when used at low doses, and include dry mouth and tiredness. With higher doses, side effects include dizziness, psycho-active effects and paranoia just to name a couple.

What Are THC And CBD's?

(THC) tetrahydrocannabinolis is a marijuana psychoactive drug. It's responsible for the "high" or euphoria feeling in people. Two drugs called dronabinol (Marinol) and nabilone (Cesamet) are considered synthetic THC forms. They are licensed by the FDA to treat symptoms like nausea and vomiting in people undergoing chemotherapy.

THC and Medical Cannabis

THC is the primary psychoactive ingredient in marijuana, THC is thought to affect the human body in different ways, including body temperature changes, heart rate, altered time perception, sedation, anxiety, spatial awareness and short-term memory.

CBD

CBD or cannabidiol is another compound that isn't psychoactive in marijuana. CBD is known to account for much of the medical benefits. CBD functions very differently than THC. For example, It takes about 100 times more CBD compared to THC to have any sort of impact on cannabinoid receptors in the body that interact with cannabinoids. Unlike THC , CBD doesn't cause any intoxication or euphoria. CBD tends to have the opposite influence of THC, in several respects. THC for example seems to increase anxiety, versus CBD which seems to reduce anxiety .

How Does Marijuana Affect the Brain?

The effect that marijuana has on the brain is complex, and varies from person to person. How good cannabis works depends on how it's being ingested. The effects are almost instantly felt when smoked, since THC reaches your bloodstream through your lungs rapidly. This triggers brain cells to release dopamine, thereby producing the euphoria feeling. Consuming cannabis makes its effects more deeply noticeable, often lasting as long as one hour or more.

Cannabinoid Receptors

Cannabinoid receptors THC and CBD are located in human cells and include numerous elements that help maintain stability within the body despite changes in the environment of the body, a term known as homeostasis. The principal receptors of cannabinoids are called CB1 and CB2 .

- **CB1 Receptors**

CB1 receptors has an affect that seems to influence the understanding of learning, motor movement, memory, as well as pain. Most CB1 receptors reside in the brain, but there are those that can be found in the liver, thyroid, uterus, bones, and testicular nerves.

- **CB2 Receivers**

CB2 receptors are also found in the brain, but play an important role in human reproduction from an embryonic development perspective. Cannabinoids act like receptors to reduce gastrointestinal inflammation and other medical conditions.

Cannabinoids and Endocannabinoids

Endocannabinoids perform a wide variety of protein synthesis-related activities, from nursing to growth to reacting to injuries. The marijuana cannabinoids interfere with the normal control of different chemicals in the body, including dopamine.

Medical Uses of THC:

THC has been shown to help AIDS patients increase their appetite. The synthetic THC medication Marinol, was approved by the U.S. Food and Drug Administration in 1985 for this purpose. Marinol has been shown to help stimulate the appetite in patients and reduce nausea and vomiting as well.

Other Medical Uses of THC

THC may be a helpful medical treatment. Here are a few of the potential medical benefits of THC:

- ✓ Inflammation reduction
- ✓ Pain reduction and discomfort
- ✓ Improving muscle control problems

Medical Uses of CBD

CBD is a non-psychoactive cannabinoid found in cannabis. Several other medical applications have been proposed for CBD, including but not limited to conditions such as Alzheimer's disease, multiple sclerosis (MS), stroke, and Parkinson's disease, in addition to pain relief for conditions such as cancer, schizophrenia, MS, rheumatoid arthritis, Parkinson's disease, (PTSD) post-traumatic stress disorder, and treatment for drug addiction like morphine and heroin.

Medical Marijuana Side Effects (Short Term)

With the many health benefits that medical marijuana provides, there are potential side effects to consider. In the short-term, medical marijuana can play a role in disrupting short-term memory, and can have a negative impact on the ability to make decisions, and can also cause a patient to feel excited, relaxed, anxious or even sleepy.

Medical Marijuana Side Effects (Long Term)

In addition to the short-term side effects, medical marijuana patients can also experience long-term side effects as well. Some of these side effects may include respiratory problems like lung infections, frequent or prolonged coughs, as well as anxiety, depression, suicidal thoughts and lack of energy.

Is Marijuana Addictive?

This question has been fiercely debated for years. There is no cut and dried definition of marijuana addiction, but (WHO) World Health Organization has defined criteria for cannabis dependency. In order to be considered marijuana-dependent by (WHO), a person must be an active user and meet three or more of the following requirements below.

The Marijuana user:

Someone who has a strong desire or compulsion to take cannabis, or has trouble controlling when and how they take cannabis, and how much they take. A user experiences withdrawal when attempting to reduce or stop the use of the drug, and requires more marijuana to get the same results.

Marijuana dependency rates are lower than other common drug addictions. Cannabis dependency was measured at about 9%, compared with 32% for nicotine, 23% for heroin, and 15% for alcohol as an overall comparison. However, when use starts in puberty, the chance of marijuana abuse climbs to 16%.

Different Ways of Using Medical Marijuana

There are three ways of using marijuana as medicine. 1. eating it, 2. breathing it in, or 3. rubbing it on the skin.

Ingesting Medical Cannabis/Marijuana

Cannabis can be taken in various edible forms. It can be baked into treats like brownies or cookies, infused into beverages, or prepared in pill form like the drugs mentioned in the previous page. When medical marijuana is developed as food or beverge, it is often considered "edible."

Upon ingesting medical marijuana, it usually takes about 30 to 60 minutes to start feeling the effects. Usually, these effects peak in two to three hours. Because of that, patients sometimes drink more than they intended. The results often last for longer when consumed with medicinal marijuana, often lasting as long as ten or more hours.

THC edibles can take many forms, including cupcakes, cookies, chocolate, hard candies, jerky, salads, and burgers.

Breathing Medical Cannabis

Smoking cannabis causes many of the same dangers as smoking cigarettes. Regular marijuana smokers can get more common upper respiratory infections, excess mucus, and persistent cough. Marijuana smoke contains some of the same cancer causing chemicals as cigarette smoke, and several marijuana smoking studies have not indicated what the level of risk is for lung cancer.

Though marijuana smoke is often held in the lungs for much longer than cigarette smoke (sometimes for 10-15 seconds), this practice is not beneficial and may be harmful. One analysis showed no distinction between a research group holding 20 seconds of marijuana smoke, another holding 10 seconds of smoke and a third group holding no smoke in their lungs at all.

Another, more recent method of cannabis digestion is through vaporizers. Some studies have shown vaporizing ("vaping") marijuana can reduce potentially harmful tar and cause less respiratory symptoms than traditional cannabis smoking. Another research, however, found that vaporizing marijuana has produced more dangerous levels of toxic ammonia that can cause asthma and can irritate lungs.

Applying Marijuana Topically

One of the least popular ways of using medical marijuana is as a topical patch, ointment or salve. Topical cannabis has some advantages over other uses. It is released directly into the bloodstream by the skin, meaning it does not break down by the stomach, making it more effective. The topical use of cannabis often reduces the harm caused by inhalation.

Where Medical Marijuana Is Legal

In 1996, California voters passed the nation's first laws to legalize medical marijuana. Since the passing of that law, all but eight States have legalized some form of medical marijuana.

Since laws vary from state to state, some states provide for the use of CBD as a medical treatment only. Others ban smoking cannabis but otherwise allow it to be consumed. Sales of medicinal and recreational marijuana have been approved by several states.

Under federal law, the sale, use and possession and distribution of marijuana remains a serious offense. According the Department of Justice, the Office of National Drug Control Policy, is committed to enforcing the Controlled Substances Act in compliance with the Congress' decision that marijuana is a dangerous drug."

How do you get medical marijuana?

Shops/stores, also called dispensaries, sell marijuana products in a variety of ways in states where medicinal marijuana is legal. Medical marijuana is sold in many edible forms, such as candies, cookies, oils, and extracts. Dispensaries that sell medical marijuana need a medical card before the products are sold to individuals. How individuals receive a medical marijuana card varies from state to state. Users that require medicinal marijuana need a licensed health-care provider prescription that needs to be presented to a dispensary before any marijuana products can be purchased.

Chapter 13 - Hiring Employees

Employee theft can cost a retail business thousands of dollars a week. It is one of those business ownership or management experiences that is all too often ignored until it happens to you. Preventing the inevitable from happening may be impossible, but putting the necessary anti-pilferage procedures in place to prevent it is one of the first things you should do as an owner of a marijuana business and grow operation. Procrastinating will only cost you money. Money that, most times, you will never see again. It's Thursday afternoon and your grow facility has been harvesting at a wonderful pace. Everything seems to be in order.

You have been trying to reconcile your inventory with your written records. To take a break from looking at numbers, you begin to organize the back room. What you find is a pile of one of your high strains of marijuana sitting on a table, definitely out of place and in an area not normally used for packaging or trimming. It's only a few steps to a door that exits to the parking lot. So that's what's been happening to your inventory, but who's the culprit? Retail store managers and owners need to take the risk of theft seriously rather than thinking that it won't ever happen to them.

This means considering that everyone working in your retail business is a potential thief. Tough as this is, it is the only way to operate, especially in a business that currently operates mostly as cash only and sells a product that is easily able to be concealed in clothes rather quickly. In the blink of an eye, hundreds, if not thousands of dollars worth of marijuana and/or hard earned cash can be picked up and stolen from right under your nose. The tragedy is that retailers usually have at their disposal tools which, if used properly, can reduce the opportunity for theft and protect the cash within the business. To help you protect your business, compiled in this section are some tips and procedures you can use in your marijuana dispensary and grow operation that can help control this kind of loss.

Hire And Train Well

Your first line of defense against employee theft is to hire honest employees. That means taking the time to check references thoroughly, including verifying dates of prior employment, and screening for past shoplifting arrests or other criminal activity. I know a crystal ball would be so much easier to tell us that the person we are considering is going to be the employee of the year, or at least not a thief, but that is unrealistic. Without spending the time to do as thorough of a background check as you can with the material you are given (usually just a resume), then you just don't know what you may end up with. Calling a few references only takes a few minutes of your time. This time is time well spent. Thirty minutes today may mean you save yourself and your business thousands of dollars tomorrow.

Train new recruits thoroughly, both in the actual job role and procedures, and in the level of integrity you expect from them. Let them know they are accountable for their actions. Set realistic rules and let them know you will always enforce them.

Be An Employer Of Choice

Employees who feel they are underpaid or treated unfairly feel justified in being dishonest or in failing to report other employees' dishonest acts. If an employee feels that they are not being treated as well as others and/or that their pay is not equivalent to other employees who work with them on the same level, in their mind they may feel they can make up this deficit in a couple of ways.

How? For starters, by not being a good employee: exhibiting poor treatment of customers or being lazy with job tasks. Another way is by stealing. Both are damaging to your business and will have a major overall effect on the daily operation and success of your retail marijuana business. Give your employees the tools to be honest. Make sure they know how to respond when friends (customers) ask them to steal or ask for discounts on marijuana your dispensary is selling. Let them know they are trusted and you are counting on them to be fair and honest, just as you are with them.

Establish Zero Tolerance

Every preventive action you take reinforces the impression that stealing from your business is a bad idea and that if they are caught they will be punished by you and the law. Consequently you must always be highly visible on the sales floor, as well as in the grow facility if you have one. Being nonexistent promotes employee theft. The old adage out of sight, out of mind comes into play. If you're not watching the till, your employees will, and will surely have their hands in it. Obviously, you can't be in all places at every waking minute of the day. The solution to this problem is to pop in every day at different times. Have no set schedule to visit the grow facility or to check inventory. Try to walk in and inspect the entire operation at both the dispensary and grow facility every time you visit, if possible. This will keep your growers, trimmers, inventory people and budtenders alert and at attention.

Tips For Eliminating Employee Theft

Establish one door as the official employee entrance and exit. Establish rules for who checks inventory, and have these checks documented: signed, time stamped, and dated. Monitor trash disposal. Keep all debris, including garbage pails, away from the building. Require at least two employees to be present at opening and closing. Handbags, backpacks, jackets, and lunch bags should be checked periodically (with employee consent).

Replace the locks and/or keys whenever an employee leaves your employment. Replace and/or change computer and alarm codes whenever an employee leaves your employment. Check places that normally do not get inspected for unusual bags or supplies whenever possible. You may never know what you may find. Light bulbs that are burned out or fixtures that are broken need to be replaced immediately.

Dark, unused areas foster employee theft. Look for unlocked or disabled doors. Check the alarm system daily. Hang signs in your place of business, including employee areas and restrooms, stating that shoplifters will be prosecuted. A camera system is mandatory in a retail business, especially in the marijuana business. Again, you can't be everywhere. Keep all employee coats, bags, lunch boxes, etc. in a designated area. Nothing personal should be in or around counters or inventory areas. Invite a law enforcement officer to walk through your place of visit for a tour. Place cameras on all doors inside and outside of the building, as well as by cash registers, front desk, trim areas, storage areas, drying areas, and grow room. Make sure cameras are visible for all to see.

The bigger the camera the better. If they see it, they will know it's there. Small capsule or hidden cameras are great from a decorating standpoint, but you want your employees and customers to know they are being watched. Check daily receipts against a list of items sold. Randomly monitor the inventory of particular items and compare with recorded sales over a period of time. If you suspect an employee of stealing, randomly audit sales by contacting customers to verify sale details. You can do this as a routine survey of customer service.

Physical Appearance/Employee Expectations:
Men: Clean, well-groomed hair within a reasonable length. No buzz cut necessary, but you should be able to see his eyes.

Women: Clean, well-groomed hair. Moderate make-up. Same standard, tasteful attire, no excessive jewelry, and conservative cleavage.

Men: For security reasons, no outer garments. A clean shirt or a tee-shirt with the store's logo. Clean, pressed pants or jeans. Jeans should not have rips, cuts, patches or tears.

Tattoos should be covered and piercings removed during business hours. Wear a visible, legible, current badge. Clear eyes and a sharp mind. Recreational usage, smoking, or consuming edibles is not permitted during working hours. EVER! This would be like a bartender/cocktail waitress drinking on the job. It is absolutely against the law. All employees MUST be over twenty-one. Bud Tender and Cannabis Consultant are good professional titles to use for your staff. Your employees are your gatekeepers, your representatives, and they should be trained and treated as such. Employees should always stand up and greet your customer in a friendly and professional manner. Be well-spoken with a calm, professional demeanor and excellent listening skills.

Hiring the right employees is as important as the inventory your store carries. One complements the other. Accomplish this and the customer's first impression will always be a positive one.

Chapter 14 - Creating a Winning Sales and Marketing Plan

Web presence and social media

Now that we're firmly planted in the twenty-first century, it's hard to imagine a business operating successfully without a website. Understanding how effective social media can help your dispensary is absolutely crucial to your marketing strategy. Once you're ready to start your company, select either a domain name or your website URL. Before you formalize the legal moniker of your dispensary, you'll want to make sure (through a site like GoDaddy.com) that that domain name is available. When you've secured your domain name, you can set up a basic webpage for free. If you've chosen to forgo a professional, you can find a variety of free templates online. These templates typically offer a step-by-step walkthrough that even the least Internet savvy person can follow.

You'll also want to consider how people will access your website. For instance, are most of your patients using smartphones? If so, you'll need to know that Flash-based sites are not viewable on iPhones. Androids, on the other hand, are Flash compatible, so the patients who use them will have no trouble accessing your site. The most important element of your website is the sign-in area. Make it a prominent part of your home page, as it's the best way to collect email addresses. This contact information will be critical as far as sending "e-mail blasts" to your database regarding specials of the week and blowout sales on products that aren't selling □uite □uickly enough. Once your business is off the ground, you can upgrade your website and make it interactive with your dispensary software program.

It's important to make clear that anyone who visits your website will will be 21 years of age or older. On your homepage (the first page anyone sees when they type in your URL), you should have two buttons, one that says "I am 21 years or older", and the other one should say "I am under 21 years of age". If a visitor who clicks on the 21 years or older, they will be permitted to enter the website. If they are in fact under 21 years or age, they will click on the under 21 years of age button, and by clicking on that button, they will not be allow to view anything on your website. Remember, you need to abide by the law, and make sure all customers are 21 years of age or older.

Patients can book appointments online, interact with you, and send feedback on what they love about your business and what they'd like to see improved. You might also create a section for the products you're promoting this week (the ones you have a surplus of, perhaps, at a reduced price!) and links to Instagram or other social media platfortms for sharing photos of your lively budtenders. Create a calendar of events that will draw people into your store and make them want to keep checking your site for new and greater promotions. Ideally, your site will be a great vehicle for bringing in business. That's why it's crucial to update it often and respond to feedback in a timely manner. It's the best way to start developing a loyal client base.

A common concern among business owners is figuring out a way to get their site on the main page of Google results. The average person searching only scrolls through the first two pages of suggested links before clicking a page that is closest to what they are looking for. Clearly being at or near the top of a search is important. Here's where Search Engine Optimization (SEO) is very important. In most cases, a company's search position is a major factor. For dispensaries, however, being at forefront of an SEO is less critical. Your website is for your clientele and a more localized area than a chain company. Your clientele will find you by local advertising, personal promoting, and, most crucially, word of mouth. That's not to say that SEO results aren't important, and you should absolutely list your dispensary in as many online directories as possible, including Google, Bing, and Yahoo map services.

From a search standpoint, this will equate to a major payoff. If you decide it's worth the effort to bring your dispensary to the top of the SEO, you have two types of websites to choose between. First, the traditional website: it sits there until someone clicks on it. You can climb the SEO ladder by paying Google (or any search engine) to let you appear at the top of the links, a position you'll pay for per each click you receive. If Google charges you $1 per click, and you receive 10,000 clicks in a month, you'd have to pay $10,000. For the average dispensary this is not a cost-effective approach. The other kind of website is designed through a WordPress platform, this is an online software that allows you to create a newsletter or blog type of webpage.

WordPress allows your site to be fluid, ever-changing, with constant activity. Before you hire a web designer, it's a good idea to interview several and find out how they feel about traditional versus WordPress. As often as the concepts behind Internet exposure evolve, you'll want to hear from experts in the field to evaluate who can do the best job for your individual business. Still, be sure to do a little research on your own, checking especially for SEO myths and scams.

Choosing a company that relies on poor tactics to improve your page rank will likely hurt you in the long run. Once you have your website up and running, what other online methods help bring exposure to your dispensary? In recent years Facebook, believe it or not, has become a viable advertising option. The social media site is often considered a place for primarily personal interactions, but it can also be extremely successful for businesses. You might also consider shooting short videos featuring different products and uploading them to your own YouTube channel.

Having an active, interesting Twitter account is another way you can help your dispensary go viral. In 140 characters or less, you can describe your weekly special, what's going on in your dispensary, something funny that will make your patients laugh and show them your brand has a sense of humor. You can send out tiny URLs that link to interesting articles, videos, or other content that will appeal to your followers, as well as track the number of clicks you receive.

You can also increase awareness about your dispensary by maintaining a blog. Each time you post to your blog, or to any of your social media outlets, the information goes into the "Internet universe" to be catalogued for future use. By regularly adding new content, you will increase your odds of being found online. Be sure to talk about the products you carry, especially the ones you're promoting. When a potential client searches online for one of those products, you'll want your dispensary showing up in the results!

Which One To Use?

In recent years, the biggest age group on Facebook has been forty-five to fifty-four year olds. On average, people spend forty minutes per day on the site, as opposed to one to three minutes for the typical website. This, clearly is an avenue for your business that you don't want to miss out on.

FACEBOOK - PERSONAL PAGE
Can import your contact list and allow you to search for Facebook friends for up to 5000 friends.

Blogs

Blogs are a lot like online diaries, only with less talk about breakups and a lot more about your industry and your dispensary. Great for sharing information in a less formal way. An outlet that's continuing to grow in popularity. Great for SEO. Provide an opportunity to showcase your credibility as a dispensary owner and operator. You can blog about business, inspirations, family, causes, or anything you like. A Blog page can be added to your website along with other pages like a Product page, About Us page, Contact us page, Specials page, etc.

Linkedin

Used primarily for business purposes. More professional users, which resembles more of an online business netowrking platform. You can import your contacts and search for current LinkedIn users, and you can also integrate your Twitter updates to post automatically to your LinkedIn update, as well as search by individual's name, company, title, location, etc. The "Answers" application feature in LinkedIn allows you to position yourself as an expert in the field, and the "Polls" application feature allows you to create polls and share them both on and off LinkedIn.

Twitter

A "micro-blogging" website which allows users a limit of up to 140 characters per update, and also allows for personalization of Twitter a page for branding purposes. You can group people you follow into lists, direct message (i.e. private message) individuals, ☐uickly update followers or send links to relevant information on external sites by adding a hashtag(#) before a word, you can also create keywords that are searchable within Twitter, for example #awesomedispensary by adding an at sign (@,) before someone's username, You can also reply to people publicly for example, @more_awesome_dispensary. A Twitter courtesy is to "retweet" information that others post and to follow those who follow you.

Other Tools To Consider

TweetDeck: Simultaneously updates your Facebook and Twitter feeds.

Twitterfeed: Feeds your blog posts into Facebook and Twitter
Hootsuite: Allows you to schedule posts across multiple social media channels.

Recommended practices for social media networks

Combine your various social media efforts with your website. Repurpose your blog into your social media. Drive traffic to your website via social media and capture user details, and include social media icons on your website that will link back to your social media pages.

Google My Business

I highly recommend setting up a Google My Business page. This is very important if you want to have a local presence, and be able to be found when someone does a local search to find your business. If you're reaching out to a Digital Media agency, Web Developer or SEO consultant, you need to ask them how deep their local search expertise is, and have them show your examples of other businesses they have helped get to the first page of Google for local listings.

If you need help with SEO or website development, I recommend you reach out to Tom Dushaj at **tomdushaj@gmail.com** to walk you through the process of how to get a website set up so it drives traffic to your website and business. He can explain how Search Engine Optimization is incorporated into a website, and which keywords, links and pages need to be optimized so that your website ranks high on Google search listings.

Conclusion

If you're planning on starting a cannabis business, there are some things you need to know right from the start. You'll be responsible for taking care of everything, from understanding the sales process, ordering and stocking inventory, advertising on social media, and more.

The cannabis culture has a rich history, and as a business owner, you need to be aware of the compound's traditional and recreational history, point of interest, and people who would invest in your products.

Here are some tips that should help you understand each aspect of the business, so you can run a successful cannabis operation.

- **Differentiate your brand**

A business's individuality and competitiveness are two of the most critical factors that can determine your future in the market. Since there are several competitors in the market already, you can start by developing a strong value proposition conveying how different or unique your product's brand is.

- **Understand the legality**

For several years, cannabis has been deemed illegal by federal and state laws in the United States and several other countries. This is mostly because of its recreational and mind-altering effects. CBD, which is one of the compounds of the cannabis Sativa plant, has also faced similar legal restrictions in the past. With the introduction of the Farm Bill in 2018, CBD products have gained significant ground in the United States. While this hemp-derived product has been said to alleviate pain, anxiety, depression, and many other health-related problems, CBD products have gained a considerable amount of popularity as well.

- **Utilize influencer marketing**

In the cannabis sector, marketing and promoting across social media is not allowed, meaning you can't place paid advertisements for cannabis products.

However, you can circumvent this problem by working with several influencers on platforms like YouTube, Twitch, and Instagram.

Such influencers have a massive network of followers that span across a wide demographic area. This makes their platforms even more beneficial to your business. So, when you plan on promoting your products through social media platforms, collaborate with a known influencer. With their help, your brand can reach a colossal network of followers all around the world.

- **Try new avenues to promote your cannabis business**

Other than social media, there are many different avenues where you can boost your cannabis business. You can start by sending your brand ambassadors to events like Hempcon to promote your products and concepts. Not only will this process help you in reaching new customers, but it will also provide more exposure to a new market.

- ## Follow all local, state and federal laws

In recent years, many CBD businesses have received shut down notices and warning letters from United States regulating bodies. So, it's always better to comply with laws and regulations that govern the cannabis industry. It's better to be safe than sorry.

- ## Be creative

One way to be creative with your cannabis business is by establishing loyalty programs. Not only does this provide an incentive for your customers to keep buying from you, but it also helps in spreading awareness about your brand.

Finally, from understanding the market and legalities, to a short and long-term influencer strategy, to exploring further avenues to sell, growing a cannabis business requires a lot of commitment.

Lastly, make sure that you adhere to every state's regulatory laws, and always conduct yourself in a professional and ethical manner. Following these practices will lead you down the path of a successful cannabis business.

www.ingramcontent.com/pod-product-compliance
Lightning Source LLC
Chambersburg PA
CBHW071444130726
47997CB00006B/2226